M000159556

Felted Knit Amigurumi

HOW TO KNIT, FELT AND CREATE ADORABLE PROJECTS

WE'RE CUTE
&
WE KNOW IT!

CINCINNATI, OHIO

Felted Knit Amigurumi *by Lisa Eberhart*

HOW TO KNIT, FELT AND CREATE ADORABLE PROJECTS

contents

?!?!

WHAT DOES A PUPPY CALL HIS FATHER?

PAW!

introduction

Because amigurumi are so often designed for crochet, many knitters feel left out when it comes to making these small, adorable creatures. The designs in this book are perfect for those who feel there just aren't enough knitted amigurumi out there. Not only that, but these fun little creations are also felted, which gives them a soft, solid look that you won't get with most other amigurumi.

Knitting these amigurumi is a great way to use up small bits of wool yarn from your stash or the odd ball of yarn that wouldn't normally go far on its own. With a little colored wool, stuffing and some felt, you can have one of these adorable amigurumi made in just a few hours.

This book has all kinds of amigurumi, from animals to food to household items. There's something here for everyone. And best of all, they'll make fantastic gifts for anyone who appreciates the power of cute! Knit a collection of cacti for a friend or a bundle of kittens for a relative. There's even a robot for the more technologically inclined. So, have fun and share the joy of amigurumi with everyone you know!

BAD HAIR DAY!

I FEEL KNITTY, OH SO KNITTY

the projects

Some projects in this book are made all as one piece and then felted while others are made in pieces, felted and then attached. Either way, the assembly diagrams should make it easy to figure out how the parts fit together.

The patterns are made with recommended colors, but don't let that stop you from trying variations! If you'd prefer a black bunny, a purple blender or a blueberry ice cream sundae, then give those other colors a try. Variations can make the same project exciting over and over again.

CHAPTER ONE

pets

⭐ finished size

Approximately 4" (10.2cm) tall, depending on the yarn used and the amount of felting

⭐ materials list

Yarn

100% wool, worsted weight

Color A: White, 25 yd. (22.8m)

Color B: Brown, 25 yd. (22.8m)

Other supplies

Size 10 US (6mm) knitting needles

Felt (black)

Embroidery floss (black, white, and brown)

Yarn needle

Embroidery needle

Polyester fiberfill

Polyester pellets, approximately 1 oz. (28g)

Cotton yarn

⭐ stitches & techniques

Cast on	Ladder stitch
Bind off	Appliqué stitch
Knit	French knot
Purl	Straight stitch
Make one (M1)	Whipstitch
K2TOG	Backstitch
Pick up stitches	
Felting	

⭐ pattern

EYE
cut 2

instructions

Head

Beginning at the back of the neck, cast on 12 stitches in Color A.

Row 1: Knit.

Row 2 and all even rows: Purl.

Row 3: K1, (M1, K1) 10 times, K1 (22 sts).

Row 5: K1, (M1, K2) 10 times, K1 (32 sts).

Row 7: Knit.

Row 9: Knit.

Row 11: K1, (K2TOG, K1) 10 times, K1 (22 sts).

Row 13: K1, (K2TOG) 10 times, K1 (12 sts).

Row 15: K1, (K2TOG) 5 times, K1 (7 sts).

Cut the yarn, leaving an 8" (20.3cm) tail. Insert a yarn needle through the remaining stitches and pull tight to close. Weave in the ends.

Body

With right sides facing, join the Color A yarn at the edge of the neck. Pick up and knit 11 stitches.

Row 1 and all odd rows: Purl.

Row 2: K1, (M1, K2) 5 times (16 sts).

Row 4: K1, (M1, K3) 5 times (21 sts).

Row 6: Knit.

Row 8: Knit.

Row 10: (K1, K2TOG) 7 times (14 sts).

Row 12: K1, (K2TOG) 6 times, K1 (8 sts).

Cut the yarn, leaving an 8" (20.3cm) tail. Insert a yarn needle through the remaining stitches and pull tight to close. With the body and the head inside out, whipstitch the seams with matching yarn, leaving a 1½" (3.8cm) opening in the back of the head. Weave in the ends on the wrong side. Turn right side out.

diagram 1

Face and Body Markings (Make 2)

Cast on 14 stitches in Color B.

Row 1: Knit.

Row 2: Purl.

Row 3: K1, (K2TOG) 6 times, K1 (8 sts).

Cut the yarn, leaving a 4" (10.2cm) tail. Insert a yarn needle through the remaining stitches and pull tight to close. Weave in the ends. Using matching yarn and an appliqué stitch, attach the face and body markings as shown in Diagram 1 *before* felting.

Ear (Make 2)

Beginning at the bottom of the ear, cast on 12 stitches in Color B.

Rows 1-11 (odd only): Knit.

Rows 2 -14 (even only): Purl.

Row 13: K2, K2TOG, K4, K2TOG, K2 (10 sts).

Row 15: K2TOG, K1, (K2TOG) 2 times, K1, K2TOG (6 sts).

Cut the yarn, leaving an 8" (20.3cm) tail. Insert a yarn needle through the remaining stitches and pull tight. Fold in half along the selvedge and whipstitch, leaving the bottom cast-on edge open. Weave in the ends. The ears will be felted separately and attached later.

Tail

Beginning at the bottom of the tail, cast on 6 stitches in Color B.

Row 1: Knit.

Row 2 and all even rows: Purl.

Row 3: K1, M1, K2TOG (2 times), M1, K1 (6 sts).

Row 5: K2TOG, M1, K2, M1, K2TOG (6 sts).

Row 6: Purl.

Cut the yarn, leaving an 8" (20.3cm) tail. Insert a yarn needle through the remaining stitches and pull tight to close. Fold in half along the selvedge and whipstitch, leaving the bottom cast-on edge open. Weave in the ends. The tail will be felted separately and attached later.

Finishing your puppy

Felting

Before you felt your puppy, work in all the yarn ends on the wrong side. Check your knitting for any holes and stitch them together loosely with matching yarn. With colorfast cotton yarn, baste to close the opening on the back. Follow the instructions under Felting Techniques to felt your puppy.

Shaping

Remove the cotton yarn from the opening at the back of the head and stuff firmly with fiberfill while damp. Mold the pieces into shape as shown in Diagram 1. The puppy's head should be shaped so that it is wider than it is tall. Shape the tail into a tube. When you are happy with the shapes, let the pieces dry overnight.

Stuffing

When completely dry, remove the temporary stuffing. Fill the bottom loosely with polyester pellets as shown in Diagram 1. Stuff the head firmly with fresh fiberfill. Use white embroidery floss and a ladder stitch to close the opening on the back. Thread the yarn through the bottom to the back of the neck and pull to create a small indentation at the base. Repeat two to three times.

Attaching Parts

Following Diagram 1, use one strand of matching embroidery floss and the ladder stitch to attach the ears and tail as shown.

Embroidery

Cut two eyes from black felt as well as a rounded trapezoid for the nose. Separate one strand from the black embroidery floss and attach the eyes and nose using the appliqué stitch as shown in Embroidery Techniques. Using three strands of white embroidery floss, make a French knot and a straight stitch for the highlights of each eye. Using three strands of black embroidery floss, backstitch the mouth.

detail of eyes

puppy variation

✪ finished size

Approximately 4" (10.2cm) tall, depending on the yarn used and the amount of felting

✪ materials list

yarn

100% wool, worsted weight

Color A: White, 20 yd. (18.2m)

Color B: Gray, 20 yd. (18.2m)

Other supplies

Size 10 US (6mm) knitting needles

Felt (pink, black)

Embroidery floss (pink, black, white, gray)

Yarn needle

Embroidery needle

Polyester fiberfill

Polyester pellets, approximately 1 oz. (28g)

Cotton yarn

✪ stitches & techniques

Cast on

Bind off

Knit

Purl

Make one (M1)

K2TOG

K3TOG

P2TOG

Pick up stitches

Felting

Ladder stitch

Appliqué stitch

French knot

Straight stitch

Whipstitch

Backstitch

✪ pattern

EYE

cut 2

rag doll kitten

instructions

Head

Beginning at the back of the neck, cast on 12 stitches in Color A.

Row 1: Knit.

Rows 2, 4 and 6: Purl.

Row 3: K1, (M1, K1) 10 times, K1 (22 sts).

Row 5: K1, (M1, K2) 10 times, K1 (32 sts).

Row 7: Knit.

Continuing in Color B:

Rows 8, 10, 12 and 14: Purl.

Row 9: Knit.

Row 11: K1, (K2TOG, K1) 10 times, K1 (22 sts).

Row 13: K1, (K2TOG) 10 times, K1 (12 sts).

Row 15: K1, (K2TOG) 5 times, K1 (7 sts).

Cut the yarn, leaving an 8" (20.3cm) tail. Insert a yarn needle through the remaining stitches and pull tight to close. Weave in the ends.

Body

With right sides facing, join the Color A yarn at the edge of the neck. Pick up and knit 11 stitches.

Row 1 and all odd rows: Purl.

Row 2: K1, (M1, K2) 5 times (16 sts).

Row 4: K1, (M1, K3) 5 times (21 sts).

Row 6: Knit.

Row 8: Knit.

Row 10: (K1, K2TOG) 7 times (14 sts).

Row 12: K1, (K2TOG) 6 times, K1 (8 sts).

Cut the yarn, leaving an 8" (20.3cm) tail. Insert a yarn needle through the remaining stitches and pull tight to close. With the body and the head inside out, whipstitch the seams with matching yarn. Leave a 1½" (3.8cm) opening in the back of the head. Turn right side out. Weave in ends.

diagram 1

Face Marking

Beginning at the bottom of the face marking, cast on 8 stitches in Color A.

Row 1: Knit.

Row 2: P1, P2TOG, P2, P2TOG, P1 (6 sts).

Row 3: K1, K2TOG, K2TOG, K1 (4 sts).

Row 4: Purl.

Row 5: K1, K2TOG, K1 (3 sts).

Row 6: Purl.

Cut the yarn, leaving a 4" (10.2cm) tail. Insert a yarn needle through the remaining stitches and pull tight to close. Weave in the ends. Using matching yarn and an appliqué stitch, attach the face marking as shown in Diagram 1 *before* felting.

Body Marking

Beginning from the bottom of the body marking, cast on 18 stitches in Color B.

Row 1: Knit.

Row 2: Purl.

Row 3: K1, K2TOG, K12, K2TOG, K1 (16 sts).

Row 4: Purl.

Row 5: K1, K2TOG, K10, K2TOG, K1 (14 sts). Bind off. Using matching yarn and an appliqué stitch, attach the body marking as shown in Diagram 1 *before* felting. Weave in the ends on the wrong side.

Ear (Make 2)

Starting from the bottom, cast on 12 stitches in Color B.

Row 1: Knit.

Row 2 and all even rows: Purl.

Row 3: K1, (K2TOG) 5 times, K1 (7 sts).

Row 5: K1, K2TOG, K3TOG, K1 (4 sts).

Cut the yarn, leaving an 8" (20.3cm) tail. Insert a yarn needle through the remaining stitches and pull tight. Trim the yarn to 1" (2.5cm) and do not weave in (this will be used for shaping). With the ears inside out, whipstitch the seams with matching yarn, leaving the bottom cast-on edge open. Turn right side out. The ears will be felted separately and attached later.

Tail

Beginning at the base of the tail, cast on 6 stitches in Color B.

Rows 1-5 (odd only): Knit.

Rows 2-6 (even only): Purl.

Continuing in Color A:

Row 7: Knit.

Row 8: Purl.

Row 9: K1, K2TOG, K2TOG, K1 (4 sts).

Cut the yarn, leaving an 8" (20.3cm) tail. Insert a yarn needle through the remaining stitches and pull tight. Whipstitch the seam with matching yarn, leaving the bottom cast-on edge open. Turn right side out. The tail will be felted separately and attached later.

Finishing your kitten

Felting

Before you felt your kitten, work in all the yarn ends on the wrong side. Check your knitting for any holes and stitch them together loosely with extra matching yarn. With colorfast cotton yarn, baste to close the opening on the back. Follow the instructions under Felting Techniques to felt your kitten.

Shaping

Remove the cotton yarn from the opening at the back of the head and stuff firmly with fiberfill while damp. Mold the pieces into shape as shown in Diagram 1. The kitten's head should be shaped so that it is wider than it is tall. Shape the ears by using the attached yarn tail to pull them into a triangle; trim as necessary. Stuff the tail and shape into a tube. When you are happy with the shapes, let them dry overnight.

Stuffing

When completely dry, remove the temporary stuffing. Fill the bottom loosely with polyester pellets as shown in Diagram 1. Stuff the head firmly with fresh fiberfill. Using white embroidery floss and a ladder stitch, close the opening on the back. Thread the yarn through the bottom to the back of the neck. Pull to create a small indentation at the base and repeat two or three times.

Attaching Parts

Following Diagram 1, use one strand of matching embroidery floss and a ladder stitch to attach the ears and tail.

Embroidery

Cut two pieces of pink felt that are the same shape but slightly smaller than the kitten's ears. Also, cut one small triangle for the nose from pink felt and two eyes from black felt. Separate one strand of black embroidery floss and attach the eyes with an appliqué stitch. Use one strand of pink embroidery floss to appliqué the ears and nose. Using three strands of white embroidery floss, make a French knot and a straight stitch for the highlights of each eye. Using three strands of embroidery floss, backstitch the mouth.

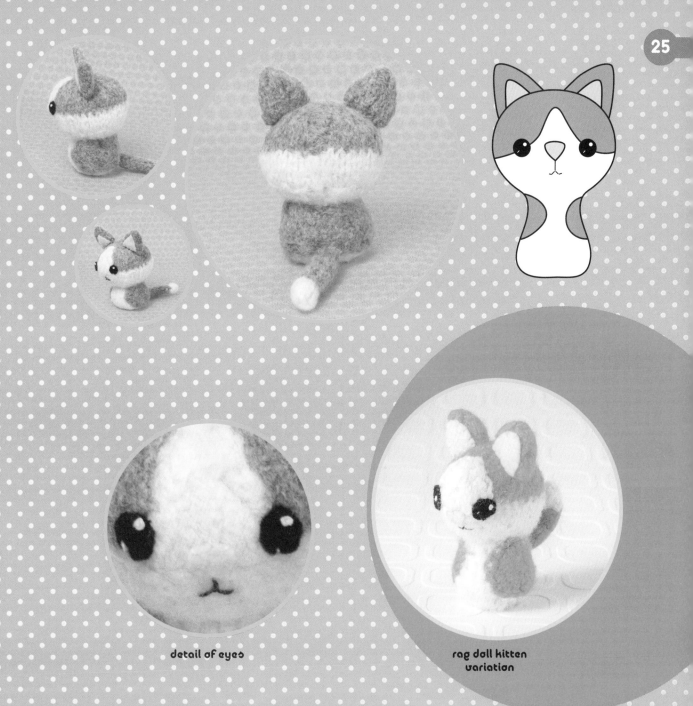

detail of eyes

rag doll kitten
variation

finished size

Approximately 4½" (11.5cm) long, depending on the yarn used and the amount of felting

materials list

yarn

100% wool, worsted weight

Color A: Orange, 35 yd. (31.9m)

Other supplies

Size 10 US (6mm) knitting needles

Felt (black)

Embroidery floss (black, white, orange)

Yarn needle

Embroidery needle

Polyester fiberfill

Cotton yarn

stitches & techniques

Cast on	Ladder stitch
Bind off	Appliqué stitch
Knit	French knot
Purl	Straight stitch
Make one (M1)	Whipstitch
K2TOG	Backstitch
Felting	

pattern

EYE

cut 2

instructions

Body

Beginning from the base of the tail, cast on 10 stitches in Color A.

Row 1: Knit.

Row 2 and all even rows: Purl.

Row 3: K1, (M1, K2) 4 times, K1 (14 sts).

Row 5: K1, (M1, K2) 6 times, K1 (20 sts).

Row 7: K1, (M1, K3) 6 times, K1 (26 sts).

Row 9: K1, (M1, K4) 6 times, K1 (32 sts).

Row 11: Knit.

Row 13: Knit.

Row 15: K1, (K2TOG, K1) 10 times, K1 (22 sts).

Row 17: K1, (K2TOG) 10 times, K1 (12 sts).

Row 19: K1, (K2TOG) 5 times, K1 (7 sts).

Row 21: K1, (K2TOG) 3 times (4 sts).

Row 23: Knit.

Bind off. Fold the mouthpiece down to row 17 and stitch to body. With body inside-out, whipstitch the seams with matching yarn, leaving a 1½" (3.8cm) opening in the bottom of body. Turn right side out. Weave in ends.

Fins (Make 3)

Cast on 12 stitches in Color A.

Row 1: Knit.

Row 2 and all even rows: Purl.

Row 3: K4, K2TOG, K2TOG, K4 (10 sts).

Row 5: K3, K2TOG, K2TOG, K3 (8 sts).

Row 7: K2, K2TOG, K2TOG, K2 (6 sts).

Row 9: K1, K2TOG, K2TOG, K1 (4 sts).

Row 11: K2TOG, K2TOG (2 sts).

Cut the yarn, leaving an 8" (20.3cm) tail. Insert a yarn needle through the remaining stitches and pull tight to close. With the fin inside out, whipstitch the seams with matching yarn. Turn right side out. Weave in the ends.

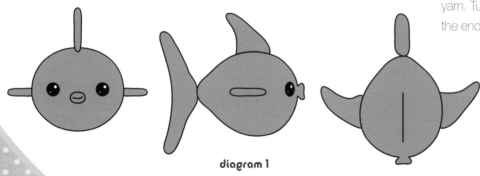

diagram 1

Tail Fin

Beginning from the bottom of the fin, cast on 40 stitches in Color A

Row 1: Knit.

Row 2 and all even rows: Purl.

Row 3: (K2TOG, K2TOG, K12, K2TOG, K2TOG) 2 times (32 sts).

Row 5: (K2TOG, K2TOG, K8, K2TOG, K2TOG) 2 times (24 sts).

Row 7: (K2TOG, K2TOG, K4, K2TOG, K2TOG) 2 times (16 sts).

Row 9: (K2TOG) 8 times (8 sts).

Row 11: (K2TOG) 4 times (4 sts). Bind off. With the fin inside out, whipstitch the seams with matching yarn. Weave in the ends on the wrong side. Turn right side out. The tail fin will be felted separately and attached later.

Finishing your goldfish

Felting

Before you felt your goldfish, work in all the yarn ends on the wrong side. Check your knitting for any holes and stitch them together loosely with matching yarn. With colorfast cotton yarn, baste to close the opening on the bottom of the fish. Follow instructions under Felting Techniques to felt your goldfish.

Shaping

Remove the cotton yarn from the opening at the bottom of the body and stuff firmly with fiberfill while damp. Mold the piece into shape as shown in Diagram 1. The goldfish's body should be shaped into a teardrop with the widest part at the front. Following Diagram 1, shape the fins. When you are happy with the shapes, let them dry overnight.

Stuffing

When completely dry, remove the temporary stuffing. Stuff the body firmly with fresh fiberfill. Use matching embroidery floss and a ladder stitch to close the opening on the bottom.

Attaching Parts

Following Diagram 1, use one strand of matching embroidery floss and a ladder stitch to attach the side and top fins and the tail fin as shown.

Embroidery

Cut two eyes from black felt. Separate one strand of black embroidery floss and attach the eyes with an appliqué stitch. Using three strands of white embroidery floss, make a French knot and a straight stitch for the highlights of each eye.

★ Finished Size

Approximately 4" (10.2cm) tall, depending on the yarn used and the amount of felting

★ Materials List

Yarn
100% wool, worsted weight

Color A: White, 32 yd. (29.1m)

Other supplies
Size 10 US (6mm) knitting needles

Felt (pink, magenta)

Embroidery floss (pink, magenta, black, white)

Yarn needle

Embroidery needle

Polyester fiberfill

Polyester pellets, approximately 1 oz. (28g)

Cotton yarn

★ Stitches & Techniques

Cast on	Ladder stitch
Bind off	Appliqué stitch
Knit	French knot
Purl	Straight stitch
Make one (M1)	Whipstitch
K2TOG	Backstitch
Pick up stitches	
Felting	

★ Pattern

EYE

cut 2

albino bunny

instructions

Head

Beginning at the back of the neck, cast on 12 stitches in Color A.

Row 1: Knit.

Row 2 and all even rows: Purl.

Row 3: K1, (M1, K1) 10 times, K1 (22 sts).

Row 5: K1, (M1, K2) 10 times, K1 (32 sts).

Rows 7 & 9: Knit.

Row 11: K1, (K2TOG, K1) 10 times, K1 (22 sts).

Row 13: K1, (K2TOG) 10 times, K1 (12 sts).

Row 15: K1, (K2TOG) 5 times, K1 (7 sts).

Cut the yarn, leaving an 8" (20.3cm) tail. Insert a yarn needle through the remaining stitches and pull tight to close.

Body

With right sides facing, join the yarn at the edge of the neck. Pick up and knit 11 stitches.

Row 1 and all odd rows: Purl.

Row 2: K1, (M1, K2) 5 times (16 sts).

Row 4: K1, (M1, K3) 5 times (21 sts).

Row 6 & 8: Knit.

Row 10: (K1, K2TOG) 7 times (14 sts).

Row 12: K1, (K2TOG) 6 times, K1 (8 sts).

Cut the yarn, leaving an 8" (20.3cm) tail. Insert a yarn needle through the remaining stitches and pull tight to close. With the body and the head inside out, whipstitch the seams with matching yarn, leaving a 1½" inch (3.8cm) opening in the back of the head. Turn right side out. Weave in the ends.

Ear (Make 2)

Beginning from the bottom, cast on 9 stitches.

Rows 1, 3 and 5: Knit.

Row 2 and all even rows: Purl.

Row 7: (K1, M1, K3, M1) 2 times, K1 (13 sts).

Rows 9 & 11: Knit.

Row 13: (K1, K2TOG) 4 times, K1 (9 sts).

Cut the yarn, leaving an 8" (20.3cm) tail. Insert a yarn needle through the remaining stitches and pull tight. With the ears inside out, whipstitch the seams with matching yarn, leaving the bottom cast-on edge open. Turn right side out. The ears will be felted separately and attached later.

Tail

Beginning from the bottom on the wrong side, cast on 8 stitches.

Row 1 and all odd rows: Purl.

Row 2: K1, (M1, K1) 6 times, K1 (14 sts).

Row 4: Knit.

Row 6: K1, (K2TOG) 6 times, K1 (8 sts).

Cut the yarn, leaving an 8" (20.3cm) tail. Insert a yarn needle through the remaining stitches and pull tight. With the tail inside out, whipstitch the seam with matching yarn, leaving the bottom cast-on edge open. Turn right side out. The tail will be felted separately and attached later.

diagram 1

Finishing your bunny

Felting

Before you felt your bunny, work in all the yarn ends on the wrong side. Check your knitting for any holes and stitch them together loosely with matching thread. With colorfast cotton yarn, baste to close the opening on the back. Follow the instructions under Felting Techniques to felt your bunny.

Shaping

Remove the cotton yarn from the opening at the back of the head and stuff firmly with fiberfill while damp. Mold into shape as shown in Diagram 1. The bunny's head should be shaped so that it is wider than it is tall. Shape the ears into teardrops as shown in Diagram 1. Stuff the tail firmly and shape into a sphere. When you are happy with the shapes, let them dry overnight.

Stuffing

When it is completely dry, remove the temporary stuffing. Fill the bottom loosely with polyester pellets as shown in Diagram 1. Stuff the head firmly with fresh fiberfill. Use white embroidery floss and a ladder stitch to close the opening. Thread the yarn through the bottom to the back of the neck and pull to create a small indentation at the base. Repeat two or three times.

Attaching Parts

Following Diagram 1, use one strand of white embroidery floss and a ladder stitch to attach the ears and tail as shown.

Embroidery

Cut two pink felt pieces the same shape but smaller than your bunny's ears. Also, cut one small triangle for the nose from pink felt and two eyes from magenta felt. Separate one strand of magenta embroidery floss and attach the eyes with an appliqué stitch. Use one strand of pink embroidery floss to appliqué the ears and nose. Using three strands of white embroidery floss, make a French knot and a straight stitch for each eye's highlights. Using three strands of black embroidery floss, backstitch the mouth.

detail of eyes

albino bunny
variation

finished size

Approximately 4" (10.2cm) tall, depending on the yarn used and the amount of felting

materials list

yarn
100% wool, worsted weight.

Color A: Natural, 30 yd. (27.3m)

Color B: White, 15 yd. (13.7m)

Color C: Brown, 10 yd. (9.1m)

Other supplies
Size 10 US (6mm) knitting needles

Felt (pink, black)

Embroidery floss (pink, black, white, brown, natural)

Yarn needle

Embroidery needle

Polyester fiberfill

Polyester pellets, approximately 1 oz. (28g)

Removable stitch markers

Cotton yarn

stitches & techniques

Cast on	Ladder stitch
Bind off	Appliqué stitch
Knit	French knot
Purl	Straight stitch
Make one (M1)	Whipstitch
K2TOG	Backstitch
Pick up stitches	
Felting	

patterns

EYE   NOSE

cut 2   cut 1

instructions

Head

Beginning at the back of the head, cast on 8 stitches in Color A.

Row 1: K1, (M1, K1) 6 times, K1 (14 sts).

Row 2 and all even rows: Purl.

Row 3: K1, (M1, K2) 6 times, K1 (20 sts).

Row 5: K1, place marker on first stitch, (M1, K3) 6 times, K1, place marker on last stitch (26 sts).

Row 7: K1, (K2TOG) 2 times, K16, (K2TOG) 2 times, K1 (22 sts).

Row 9: Knit.

Row 11: (K1, M1) 2 times, K18, (M1, K1) 2 times (26 sts).

Row 13: K1, place marker on first stitch, (K2TOG, K2) 6 times, K1, place marker on last stitch (20 sts).

Continuing with Color B:

Row 15: Knit.

Row 17: K1, (K2TOG, K1) 6 times, K1 (14 sts).

Row 19: Knit.

Row 21: K1, (K2TOG) 6 times, K1 (8 sts).

Row 23: K1, (K2TOG) 3 times, K1 (5 sts).

Cut the yarn, leaving an 8" (20.3cm) tail. Insert a yarn needle through the remaining stitches and pull tight to close. With the head inside out, use matching yarn to whipstitch the seam closed from the nose to the neck (Row 13). Weave in the ends.

Body

With right sides facing, join Color A at the edge of the neck by picking up and knitting 11 stitches between the stitch markers placed in Row 5 of the head.

Row 1 and all odd rows: Purl.

Row 2: K1, (M1, K2) 5 times (16 sts).

Row 4: K1, (M1, K3) 5 times (21 sts).

Row 6: Knit.

Row 8: K1, (M1, K4) 5 times (26 sts).

Row 10: Knit.

Row 12: Knit.

Row 14: K1, (K2TOG) 12 times, K1 (14 sts.).
Row 16: K1, (K2TOG) 6 times, K1 (8 sts).
Cut the yarn, leaving an 8" (20.3m) tail. Insert a yarn needle through the remaining stitches and pull tight to close. With the body and the head inside out, whipstitch the seams with matching yarn, leaving a 1½" (3.8cm) opening in the back of the head. Turn right side out. Weave in ends.

Mask

Beginning at the top of the mask, cast on 10 stitches in Color C.
Row 1: Knit.
Row 2: Purl.
Row 3: K1, K2TOG, K4, K2TOG, K1 (8 sts).
Row 4: Purl.
Bind off. Using matching yarn and an appliqué stitch, attach the mask to the head before felting. Weave in the ends.

Chest

Beginning at the top of the chest, cast on 4 stitches in Color B.
Row 1: Knit.
Row 2 and all even rows: Purl.
Row 3: K2, M1, K2 (5 sts).
Row 5: K1, M1, K3, M1, K1 (7 sts).
Row 7: K1, K2TOG, K1, K2TOG, K1 (5 sts).
Row 9: K2TOG, K1, K2TOG (3 sts).
Cut the yarn, leaving a 4" (10.2cm) tail. Insert a yarn needle through the remaining stitches and pull tight. Using matching yarn and an appliqué stitch, attach the chest to the body. Weave in the ends.

diagram 1

Ear (Make 2)

Beginning on the wrong side, cast on 8 stitches in Color A.

Row 1: Purl.

Row 2: K1, (K1, M1, K2) 2 times, K1 (10 sts).

Cut the yarn, leaving a 4" (10.2cm) tail. Insert a yarn needle through the remaining stitches and pull tight. With the ears inside out, whipstitch the seams with matching yarn, leaving the bottom cast-on edge open. Turn right side out. The ears will be felted separately and attached later.

Tail

Beginning at the bottom of the tail, cast on 9 stitches in Color A.

Rows 1, 3 and 5: Knit.

Row 2 and all even rows: Purl.

Row 7: K2, (K2TOG) 3 times, K1 (5 sts).

Cut the yarn, leaving an 8" (20.3cm) tail. Insert a yarn needle through the remaining stitches and pull tight. With the tail inside out, whipstitch the seam with matching yarn, leaving the bottom cast-on edge open. Turn right side out. The tail will be felted separately and attached later.

Finishing your Ferret

Felting

Before you felt your ferret, work in all yarn ends on the wrong side. Check your knitting for any holes and stitch them together loosely with matching yarn. With colorfast cotton yarn, baste to close the opening on the back. Follow the instructions under Felting Techniques to felt your ferret.

Shaping

Remove the cotton yarn from the opening at the back of the head and stuff firmly with fiberfill while damp. Mold the pieces into shape as shown in Diagram 1. The ferret's head should be shaped into a teardrop with the smallest point at the nose. Shape the ears into ovals. Stuff the tail and shape it into a tube. When you are happy with the shapes, let them dry overnight.

Stuffing

When completely dry, remove the temporary stuffing. Fill the bottom loosely with polyester pellets as shown in Diagram 1. Stuff the head firmly with fresh fiberfill. Use white embroidery floss and a ladder stitch to close the opening on the back. Thread the yarn through the bottom to the back of the neck and pull to create a small indentation at the base. Repeat two to three times.

Attaching Parts

Following Diagram 1, use one strand of matching embroidery floss and a ladder stitch to attach the ears and tail.

Embroidery

Cut two pieces of pink felt the same shape as the ears but slightly smaller. Also cut one nose from pink felt and two eyes from black felt. Separate one strand of black embroidery floss and attach the eyes with an appliqué stitch. Use one strand of pink embroidery floss to appliqué the ears and nose. Using three strands of white embroidery floss, make a French knot and a straight stitch for the highlights of each eye. Using three strands of embroidery floss, backstitch the mouth.

detail of eyes

ferret variation

finished size

Approximately 3½" (8.9cm) tall, depending on the yarn used and the amount of felting

materials list

Yarn

100% wool, worsted weight

Color A: White, 20 yd. (18.2m)

Color B: Rust, 20 yd. (18.2m)

Color A: Black, 15 yd. (13.7m)

Other supplies

Size 10 US (6mm) knitting needles

Felt (pink, black)

Embroidery floss (pink, black, white)

Yarn needle

Embroidery needle

Polyester fiberfill

Polyester pellets, approximately 1 oz. (28g)

Cotton yarn

stitches & techniques

Knit

Purl

Make one (M1)

K2TOG

Pick up stitches

Knit with multiple colors

Felting

Ladder stitch

Applique stitch

French knot

Straight stitch

Whipstitch

Backstitch

pattern

EYE

cut 2

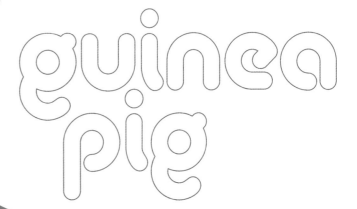

instructions

Head

Beginning at the back of the neck, cast on 20 stitches in Color A.

Row 1: Knit.

Rows 2, 4 and 6: Purl.

Row 3: K1, (M1, K3) 6 times, K1 (26 sts).

Row 5: K1, (M1, K2) 12 times, K1 (38 sts).

Row 7: Knit

Continuing in Color B:

Rows 8, 10, 12 and 14: Purl.

Row 9: Knit.

Row 11: K1, (K2TOG, K1) 12 times, K1 (26 sts).

Row 13: K1, (K2TOG) 12 times, K1 (14 sts).

Row 15: K1, (K2TOG) 6 times, K1 (8 sts).

Cut the yarn, leaving an 8" (20.3cm) tail. Insert a yarn needle through the remaining stitches and pull tight to close. Weave in the ends.

Body

With right sides facing, join the Color A yarn at the edge of the neck. Pick up and knit 19 stitches.

Rows 1 & 3: Purl.

Row 2: Knit.

Continuing in Color C:

Row 4: K1, (M1, K3) 6 times (25 sts).

Rows 5, 7, 9 and 11: Purl.

Row 6 and 8: Knit.

Row 10: K1, (K2TOG) 12 times (13 sts).

Row 12: K1, (K2TOG) 6 times (7 sts).

Cut the yarn, leaving an 8" (20.3cm) tail. Insert a yarn needle through the remaining stitches and pull tight to close. With the body and the head inside out, whipstitch the seams with matching yarn, leaving a 1½" (3.8cm) opening in the back of the head. Turn right side out. Weave in the ends.

Face Markings

Beginning from the bottom of the face marking, cast on 6 stitches in Color A.

Row 1: Knit.

Row 2 and all even rows: Purl.

Row 3: K1, K2TOG, K2TOG, K1 (4 sts).

Row 5: Knit.

Bind off purlwise. Using matching yarn and an appliqué stitch, attach the face marking to the head and the body prior to felting. Weave in the ends.

Ear (Make 2)

Beginning on the wrong side, cast on 8 stitches in Color B.

Row 1: Purl.

Row 2: K1, (K1, M1, K2) 2 times, K1 (10 sts). Cut the yarn, leaving a 4" (10.2cm) tail. Insert a yarn needle through the remaining stitches and pull tight. With the ears inside out, whipstitch the seams with matching yarn, leaving the bottom cast-on edge open. Turn right side out. The ears will be felted separately and attached later.

diagram 1

finishing your guinea pig

Felting

Before you felt your guinea pig, work in all yarn ends on the wrong side. Check your knitting for any holes and stitch them together loosely with matching yarn. With colorfast cotton yarn, baste to close the opening on the back. Follow the instructions under Felting Techniques to felt your guinea pig.

Shaping

Remove the cotton yarn from the opening at the back of the head and stuff firmly with fiberfill while damp. Mold the shapes as shown in Diagram 1. The Guinea Pig's head should be shaped so that it is wider than it is tall. Shape the ears into ovals as shown in Diagram 1. When you are happy with the shapes, let them dry overnight.

Stuffing

When completely dry, remove the temporary stuffing. Fill the bottom loosely with poly pellets as shown in Diagram 1. Stuff the head firmly with fresh fiberfill. Using matching embroidery floss and a ladder stitch, close the opening at the back. Thread the yarn through the bottom to the back of the neck and pull to create a small indentation at the base. Repeat two or three times.

Attaching Parts

Following Diagram 1, use one strand of white embroidery floss and a ladder stitch to attach the ears as shown.

detail of eyes

Embroidery

From pink felt, cut two pieces the same shape as the ears but slightly smaller. Also cut one small triangle for the nose from pink felt and two eyes from black felt. Separate one strand of black embroidery floss and attach the eyes with an appliqué stitch. Use one strand of pink embroidery floss to appliqué the ears and nose. Using three strands of white embroidery floss, make a French knot and a straight stitch for each eye's highlights. Using three strands of embroidery floss, backstitch the mouth.

guinea pig variation

CHAPTER TWO

around the house

★ finished size

Approximately 5" (12.7cm) tall, depending on the yarn used and the amount of felting

★ materials list

Yarn

100% wool, worsted weight

Color A: Leaf Green, 25 yd. (22.8m)

Color C: Sand, 15 yd. (13.7m)

Color D: Magenta, 30 yd. (27.3m)

Color E: Yellow, 10 yd. (9.1m)

Other supplies

Size 10 US (6mm) knitting needles

Felt (black)

Embroidery floss (black, white, natural, pink)

Yarn needle

Embroidery needle

Polyester fiberfill

Polyester pellets, approximately 1 oz. (28g)

Cotton yarn

★ stitches & techniques

Cast on	Ladder stitch
Bind off	Appliqué stitch
Knit	French knot
Purl	Straight stitch
Make one (M1)	Backstitch
K2TOG	Whipstitch
P2TOG	
Pick up stitches	
Wrap and turn	
Felting	

★ pattern

(EYE)

cut 2

cactus

instructions

Cactus

Beginning at the back of the cactus, cast on 12 stitches in Color A.

Rows 1-31 (odd only): Knit.

Rows 2-30 (even only): Purl.

Bind off. Using contrasting yarn, mark every third row. Pick up, knit and bind off every third row to create ridges. Fold the cactus in half with right sides facing and whipstitch. Thread the yarn through each row on one side of the selvedge and pull tight. Repeat for the other side but leave a small opening for stuffing. Weave through the stitches again and fasten. Weave in the ends.

Sand

Beginning on the wrong side, cast on 38 stitches in Color B.

Row 1 and all odd rows: Purl.

Row 2: K1, (K2TOG, K1) 12 times, K1 (26 sts).

Row 4: K1, (K2TOG) 12 times, K1 (14 sts).

Row 6: K1, (K2TOG) 6 times, K1 (8 sts).

Cut the yarn, leaving a 4" (10.2cm) tail. Insert a yarn needle through the remaining stitches and pull tight. With right sides facing, whipstitch the seam with matching yarn. The sand will be felted separately and attached later.

Terracotta Pot

Beginning at the bottom rim of the pot, cast on 35 stitches in Color C.

Row 1: Knit.

Row 2: Purl.

Row 3: K1, (M1, K11) 3 times, K1 (38 sts).

Row 4: Purl.

Row 5: Purl.

Row 6: Knit.

Row 7: Purl.

Row 8: Knit.

Row 9: P1, (P2TOG, P10) 3 times, P1 (35 sts).

Row 10: Knit.

detail of eyes

Row 11: Purl.

Row 12: Knit.

Row 13: Purl.

Row 14: K1, (K2TOG, K9) 3 times, K1 (32 sts).

Row 15: Purl.

Row 16: Knit.

Row 17: Purl.

Row 18: Knit.

Row 19: P1, (P2TOG, P8) 3 times, P1 (29 sts).

Row 20: Knit.

Row 21: Purl.

Row 22: Knit.

Row 23: Purl.

Row 24: K1, (K2TOG, K7) 3 times, K1 (26 sts).

Row 25: Purl.

Row 26: K1, (K2TOG) 12 times, K1 (14 sts).

Row 27: Purl.

Row 28: K1, (K2TOG) 6 times, K1 (8 sts). Cut the yarn, leaving an 8" (20.3cm) tail. Insert a yarn needle through the remaining stitches and pull tight. Whipstitch the seams with matching yarn, leaving the bottom cast-on edge open. Weave in the ends on the wrong side. The terracotta pot will be felted separately and attached later.

diagram 1

Flower Petals

Beginning in the middle, cast on 8 stitches in Color D.

Row 1: K6, wrap and turn.

Row 2: Knit.

Row 3: Bind off 3, K2, wrap and turn.

Row 4: Knit. Cast on 3 sts.

Row 5: K4, wrap and turn.

Row 6: Knit.

Row 7: Bind off 3, knit.

Row 8: Knit. Cast on 3 sts.

Repeat rows 1-8 five more times. Bind off. Whipstitch the seams with matching yarn and weave in the ends. The flower petals will be felted separately and attached later.

Flower Center

Beginning at the bottom of the flower, cast on 13 stitches in Color E.

Row 1: Knit.

Row 2: Purl.

Row 3: K1, (K2TOG) 6 times (7 sts).

Cut the yarn, leaving a 4" (10.2cm) tail. Insert a yarn needle through the remaining stitches and pull tight. Whipstitch the seam with matching yarn and weave in the ends. The flower center will be felted separately and attached later.

Finishing your cactus

Felting

Before you felt your cactus, work in all the yarn ends on the wrong side. Check your knitting for any holes and stitch them together loosely with matching yarn. Follow the instructions under Felting Techniques to felt your cactus.

Shaping

Stuff the cactus and pot firmly with fiberfill while damp. Mold them into shape as shown in Diagram 1. The cactus should be shaped so that it is wider than it is tall. Shape the sand and flower center into flat circles and the flower petals into a cup. When you are happy with the shapes, let them dry overnight.

Stuffing and Assembly

When completely dry, remove temporary stuffing. Fill the bottom of pot loosely with polyester pellets as shown in Diagram 1. Use a ladder stitch to attach the sand to the pot, stuffing firmly. Thread yarn through the bottom center of the pot to the center of the sand and pull to create a small indentation at the base. Repeat two or three times. Stuff the cactus firmly. Attach the flower petals to the flower center. Use matching embroidery floss and a ladder stitch to attach the cactus and flower as shown in Diagram 1.

Embroidery

Cut two eyes from black felt. Separate one strand of black embroidery floss and attach the eyes with an appliqué stitch. Using three strands of white embroidery floss, make a French knot and straight stitch for each eye's highlights. Using three strands of embroidery floss, backstitch the mouth.

cactus variation

⭐ Finished Size

Approximately 4½" (11.4cm) tall, depending on the yarn used and the amount of felting

⭐ Materials List

Yarn

100% wool, worsted weight

Color A: Gray, 35 yd. (31.9m)

Color B: Black, 15 yd. (13.7m)

Other supplies

Size 10 US (6mm) knitting needles

Felt (gray, green, red, blue)

Embroidery floss (blue, gray, green, red, black, white)

Yarn needle

Embroidery needle

Polyester fiberfill

Polyester pellets, approximately 1 oz. (28g)

Removable stitch markers

Cotton yarn

⭐ Stitches & Techniques

Cast on	Ladder stitch
Bind off	Appliqué stitch
Knit	French knot
Purl	Straight stitch
Make one (M1)	Backstitch
K2TOG	Whipstitch
Knit with multiple colors	
Pick up stitches	
Felting	

⭐ Patterns

EYE
cut 2

LARGE RECTANGLE
cut 1

robot

instructions

Head

Beginning at the back of the neck, cast on 14 stitches in Color A.

Row 1: Knit.

Row 2 and all even rows: Purl.

Row 3: K1, (M1, K1) 12 times, K1 (26 sts).

Row 5: K1, (M1, K2) 12 times, K1 (38 sts).

Rows 7, 9 & 11: Knit.

Row 13: K1, (K2TOG, K1) 12 times, K1 (26 sts).

Row 15: K1, (K2TOG) 12 times, K1 (14 sts).

Row 17: K1, (K2TOG) 6 times, K1 (8 sts).

Cut the yarn, leaving an 8" (20.3cm) tail. Insert a yarn needle through the remaining stitches and pull tight.

Body

With right sides facing, join the Color A yarn at the edge of the neck. Pick up and knit 13 stitches.

Row 1: Purl.

Continuing in Color B:

Row 2: Knit.

Continuing in Color A:

Row 3: Purl.

Continuing in Color B:

Row 4: Knit.

Continuing in Color A:

Row 5: Purl.

Continuing in Color B:

Row 6: K1, (M1, K2) 5 times, (M1, K1) 2 times (20 sts).

Row 7: Purl.

Row 8: Knit.

Row 9: Purl.

Row 10: K1, (M1, K3) 6 times, K1 (26 sts).

Row 11: Purl.

Row 12: Knit.

Row 13: Purl.

Row 14: K1, (K2TOG) 12 times, K1 (14 sts).

Row 15: Purl.

Row 16: K1, (K2TOG) 6 times, K1 (8 sts).

Cut the yarn, leaving an 8" (20.3cm) tail. Insert a yarn needle through the remaining stitches and pull tight. With the body and the head inside out, whipstitch the seams with matching yarn, leaving a 1½" (3.8cm) opening in the back of head. Turn right side out. Weave in the ends.

Skirt

Beginning at the top of the skirt, cast on 16 stitches in Color A.

Row 1: Knit.

Row 2: Purl.

Row 3: K1, (M1, K5) 3 times (19 sts).

Row 4: Purl.

Row 5: K1, (M1, K6) 3 times (22 sts).

Row 6: Purl.

Row 7: K1, (M1, K7) 3 times (25 sts).

Row 8: Purl.

Bind off. With the skirt inside out, whipstitch the seams with matching yarn. Turn right side out. Weave in the ends. The skirt will be felted separately and attached later.

Large Antenna (Make 2)

Starting on the wrong side, cast on 14 stitches in Color A.

Row 1: Purl.

Row 2: K1, (K2TOG) 6 times, K1 (8 sts).

Cut the yarn, leaving a 4" (10.2cm) tail. Insert a yarn needle through the remaining stitches and pull tight. With right sides facing, whipstitch the seam with matching yarn. The large antennae will be felted separately and attached later.

Small Antenna (Make 2)

Beginning on the wrong side, cast on 8 sts in Color A.

Row 1: Purl.

Row 2: Knit.

Cut the yarn, leaving a 4" (10.2cm) tail. Insert a yarn needle through the remaining stitches and pull tight. With right sides facing, whipstitch the seam with matching yarn. The small antennae will be felted separately and attached later.

diagram 1

Finishing your robot

Felting

Before you felt your robot, work in all of the yarn ends on the wrong side. Check your knitting for any holes and stitch them together loosely with matching yarn. With colorfast cotton yarn, baste to close the opening on the back. Follow the instructions under Felting Techniques to felt your robot.

Shaping

Remove the cotton yarn from the opening at the back of the head and stuff firmly with fiberfill while damp. Mold into shape as shown in Diagram 1. The robot's head should be shaped so that it is wider than it is tall. Following Diagram 1, shape the antennae into circles. When you are happy with the shapes, let them dry overnight.

Stuffing

When completely dry, remove temporary stuffing. Fill the bottom loosely with polyester pellets as shown in Diagram 1. Stuff the head firmly. Use gray embroidery floss and a ladder stitch to close the opening. Thread the yarn through the bottom to the back of the neck and pull to create a small indentation at the base. Repeat two to three times.

Attaching Parts

Following Diagram 1, use one strand of matching embroidery floss and a ladder stitch to attach the antennae as shown. Slip the skirt over the body and secure if desired.

Embroidery

Cut one control panel from the gray felt, then cut a small rectangle from red felt and a larger rectangle from green felt to fit within the control panel. Also cut two eyes from blue felt. Separate one strand of blue embroidery floss and attach the eyes with an appliqué stitch. Use one strand of matching embroidery floss to appliqué the control panel, small rectangle and large rectangle as shown in Diagram 1. Using three strands of black embroidery floss, make French knots for the screws on the control panel. Using three strands of white embroidery floss, make a French knot and a straight stitch for the highlights of each eye. Using three strands of embroidery floss, backstitch the mouth.

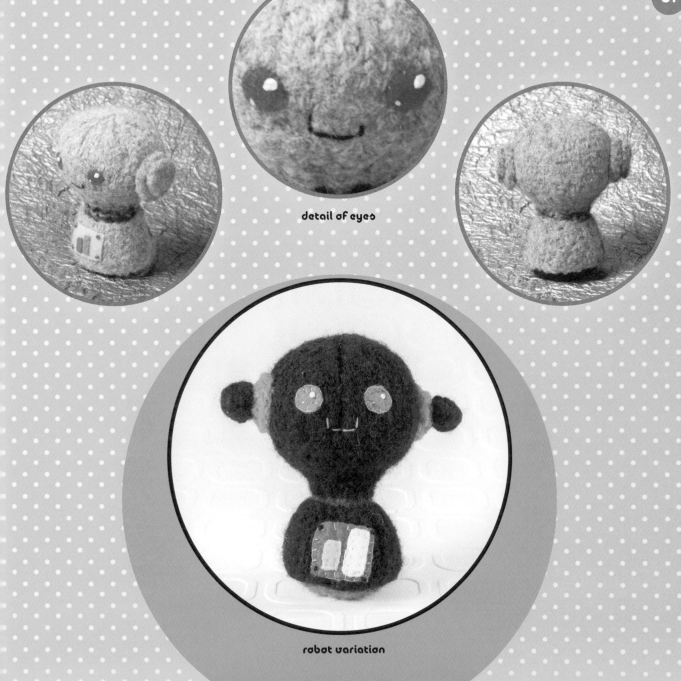

detail of eyes

robot variation

★ Finished Size

Approximately 4" (10.2cm) tall, depending on the yarn used and the amount of felting

★ Materials List

Yarn

100% wool, worsted weight

Color A: Brown, 30 yd. (27.3m)

Color B: White, 15 yd. (13.7m)

Color A: Red, 10 yd. (9.1m)

Other supplies

Size 10 US (6mm) knitting needles

Size 10 US (6mm) double-pointed needles (optional)

Felt (black)

Embroidery floss (red, black, white, brown)

Yarn needle

Embroidery needle

Polyester fiberfill

Polyester pellets, approximately 1 oz. (28g)

Cotton yarn

★ Stitches & Techniques

Cast on	Ladder stitch
Bind off	Appliqué stitch
Knit	French knot
Purl	Straight stitch
Make one (M1)	Whipstitch
K2TOG	Backstitch
Pick up stitches	
Knit with multiple colors	
Felting	

★ Pattern

EYE
cut 2

sock monkey

instructions

Head

Beginning at the back of the neck, cast on 14 stitches in Color A.

Row 1: Knit.

Row 2 and all even rows: Purl.

Row 3: K1, (M1, K1) 12 times, K1 (26 sts).

Row 5: K1, (M1, K2) 12 times, K1 (38 sts).

Rows 7, 9 and 11: Knit.

Row 13: K1, (K2TOG, K1) 12 times, K1 (26 sts).

Continuing in Color B:

Row 14: Purl.

Row 15: K1, (K2TOG) 12 times, K1 (14 sts).

Row 16: Purl.

Row 17: K1, (K2TOG) 6 times, K1 (8 sts).

Cut the yarn, leaving an 8" (20.3cm) tail. Insert a yarn needle through the remaining stitches and pull tight.

Body

With right sides facing, begin at the neck with Color A. Pick up and knit 13 stitches.

Row 1 and all odd rows: Purl.

Row 2: K1, (M1, K2) 5 times, (M1, K1) 2 times (20 sts).

Row 4: Knit.

Row 6: K1, (M1, K3) 6 times, K1 (26 sts).

Row 8: Knit.

Continuing in Color B:

Row 9: Purl.

Row 10: K1, (K2TOG) 12 times, K1 (14 sts).

Row 11: Purl.

Row 12: K1, (K2TOG) 6 times, K1 (8 sts).

Cut the yarn, leaving an 8" (20.cm) tail. Insert a yarn needle through the remaining stitches and pull tight, leaving a 1½" (3.8cm) opening in the back of the head. Weave in the ends on the wrong side.

Large Face Marking

Beginning on the wrong side, cast on 3 stitches in Color B.

Row 1 and all odd rows: Purl.

Row 2: K1, M1, K1, M1, K1 (5 sts).

Row 4: K1, M1, K3, M1, K1 (7 sts).

Row 6: K1, M1, K5, M1, K1 (9 sts).

Row 8: K1, M1, K7, M1, K1 (11 sts).

Row 10: K1, K2TOG, K5, K2TOG, K1 (9 sts).

Row 12: K1, K2TOG, K3, K2TOG, K1 (7 sts).

Row 14: K1, K2TOG, K1, K2TOG, K1 (5 sts).

Row 15: Purl.

Bind off while working K2TOG, K1, K2TOG. Using matching yarn and an appliqué stitch, attach the large face marking as shown in Diagram 1 *before* felting. Weave in the ends.

Small Face Marking

Beginning on the wrong side, cast on 3 stitches in Color C.

Row 1 and all odd rows: Purl.

Row 2: K1, M1, K1, M1, K1 (5 sts).

Row 4: K1, M1, K3, M1, K1 (7 sts).

Row 6: K1, K2TOG, K1, K2TOG, K1 (5 sts).

Row 7: Purl.

Bind off while working K2TOG, K1, K2TOG. Using matching yarn and an appliqué stitch, attach the small face marking as shown in Diagram 1 *before* felting. Weave in the ends.

Ear (Make 2)

Beginning at the bottom of the ear, cast on 8 stitches in Color A.

Row 1: K2, M1, K4, M1, K2 (10 sts).

Row 2 : Purl.

Row 3: Knit.

Row 4: Purl.

Row 5: K1, (K2TOG) 4 times, K1 (6 sts). Cut the yarn, leaving a 4" (10.2cm) tail. Insert a yarn needle through the remaining stitches and pull tight. With the ears inside out, whipstitch the seams with matching yarn, leaving the bottom cast-on edge open. Turn right side out. The ears will be felted separately and attached later.

Tail

Beginning at the bottom of the tail, cast on 4 stitches in color A.

Rows 1-7 (odd only): Knit.

Rows 2-8 (even only): Purl.

Bind off. Fold in half widthwise and whipstitch the seams with matching yarn, leaving the bottom cast-on edge open. The tail will be felted separately and attached later.

diagram 1

Finishing your sock monkey

Felting

Before you felt your sock monkey, work in all the yarn ends on the wrong side. Check your knitting for any holes and stitch them together loosely with matching yarn. With colorfast cotton yarn, baste to close the opening on the back. Follow the instructions under Felting Techniques to felt your sock monkey.

Shaping

Remove the cotton yarn from the opening at the back of the head and stuff firmly with fiberfill while damp. Mold pieces into shape as shown in Diagram 1. The sock monkey's head should be shaped so that it is wider than it is tall. Shape the ears into ovals as shown in Diagram 1. When you are happy with the shapes, let them dry overnight.

Stuffing

When completely dry, remove the temporary stuffing. Fill the bottom loosely with polyester pellets as shown in Diagram 1. Stuff the head firmly with fresh fiberfill. Use matching embroidery floss and a ladder stitch to close the opening. Thread the yarn through the bottom to the back of the neck and pull to create a small indentation. Repeat two or three times.

Attaching Parts

Use one strand of matching embroidery floss and a ladder stitch to attach the ears as shown.

Embroidery

Cut two eyes from black felt. Separate one strand of black embroidery floss and attach the eyes with an appliqué stitch. Using three strands of white embroidery floss, make a French knot and a straight stitch for each eye's highlights. Using three strands of black embroidery floss, make a French knot for each nostril and backstitch the mouth.

detail of eyes

sock monkey variation

Finished Size

Approximately 5" (12.7cm) tall, depending on the yarn used and the amount of felting

Materials List

Yarn

100% wool, worsted weight

Color A: Heather Green, 15 yd. (13.7m)

Color B: Brown, 10 yd. (9.1m)

Color C: Leaf Green, 10 yd. (9.1m)

Color D: White, 20 yd. (18.2m)

Other supplies

Size 10 US (6mm) knitting needles

Felt (black)

Embroidery floss (black, white, green, brown)

Yarn needle

Embroidery needle

Polyester fiberfill

Flexible craft foam

Polyester pellets, approximately 1 oz. (28g)

Cotton yarn

Stitches & Techniques

Cast on

Bind off

Knit

Purl

Make one (M1)

K2TOG

Pick up stitches

Felting

Ladder stitch

Appliqué stitch

French knot

Straight stitch

Pattern

EYE

cut 2

instructions

Topiary

Beginning at the bottom, cast on 8 stitches in Color A.

Row 1: Knit.

Row 2 and all even rows: Purl.

Row 3: K1, (M1, K1) 6 times, K1 (14 sts).

Row 5: K1, (M1, K1) 12 times, K1 (26 sts).

Row 7: K1, (M1, K2) 12 times, K1 (38 sts).

Row 9: Knit.

Row 11: Knit.

Row 13: Knit.

Row 15: K1, (K2TOG, K1) 12 times, K1 (26 sts).

Row 17: K1, (K2TOG) 12 times, K1 (14 sts).

Row 19: K1, (K2TOG) 6 times, K1 (8 sts).

Cut the yarn, leaving an 8" (20.3cm) tail. Insert a yarn needle through the remaining stitches and pull tight. With right sides facing, whipstitch the seam with matching yarn.

Stem

Cast on 9 stitches in Color B.

Rows 1–9 (odd only): Knit.

Rows 2–10 (even only): Purl.

Bind off. Whipstitch the seams with matching yarn, leaving the bottom and top edges open. Weave in the ends on the wrong side. The stem will be felted separately and attached later.

Moss

Beginning on the wrong side, cast on 38 stitches in Color C.

Row 1: Purl.

Row 2: K1, (K2TOG, K1) 12 times, K1 (26 sts).

Row 3: Purl.

Row 4: K1, (K2TOG) 12 times, K1 (14 sts).

Row 5: Purl.

Row 6: K1, (K2TOG) 6 times, K1 (8 sts).

Cut the yarn, leaving a 4" (10.2cm) tail. Insert a yarn needle through the remaining stitches and pull tight. With right sides facing, whipstitch the seam with matching yarn. The moss will be felted separately and attached later.

Urn

Beginning from the rim of the urn, cast on 38 stitches in Color D.

Row 1: Knit.

Row 2 and all even rows: Purl.

Row 3: K1, (K2TOG, K1) 13 times, K1 (26 sts).

Row 5: Knit.

Row 7: K1, (M1, K4) 6 times, K1 (32 sts).

Row 9: K1, (M1, K5) 6 times, K1 (38 sts).

Row 11: Knit.

Row 13: Knit.

Row 15: K1, (K2TOG, K1) 12 times, K1 (26 sts).

Row 17: K1, (K2TOG) 12 times, K1 (14 sts).

Row 19: K1, (K2TOG) 6 times, K1 (8 sts).

Cut the yarn, leaving an 8" (20.3cm) tail. Insert a yarn needle through the remaining stitches and pull tight. With right sides facing, whipstitch the seam with matching yarn. The urn will be felted separately and attached later.

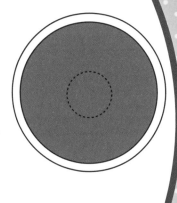

diagram 1

Finishing your topiary

Felting

Before you felt your topiary, work in all the yarn ends on the wrong side. Check your knitting for any holes and stitch them together loosely with matching thread. Follow the instructions under Felting Techniques to felt your topiary.

Shaping

Stuff the topiary and urn firmly with fiberfill while damp. Mold them into shape as shown in Diagram 1. The topiary should be shaped so that it is wider than it is tall. Shape the moss into a flat circle and the stem into a tube. When you are happy with the shapes, let them dry overnight.

Stuffing and Assembly

When completely dry, remove temporary stuffing. Fill the bottom of the urn loosely with polyester pellets as shown in Diagram 1. Use a ladder stitch to attach the moss to the pot, stuffing firmly. Thread the yarn through the bottom center of the urn to the center of the moss, then to the back and pull to create a small indentation at the base. Repeat two or three times.

Stuff the topiary firmly. Cut a piece of craft foam as tall as the stem and 3 times as wide. Curve it into a tube and insert it into the stem. Fill any remaining space with stuffing and sew one end to the moss and the other to the topiary.

Embroidery

Cut two eyes from black felt. Separate one strand of black embroidery floss and attach the eyes with an appliqué stitch. Using three strands of white embroidery floss, make a French knot and straight stitch for each eye's highlights. Using three strands of embroidery floss, backstitch the mouth.

detail of eyes

topiary variation

✪ finished size

Approximately 6" (15.2cm) tall, depending on the yarn used and the amount of felting

✪ materials list

yarn

100% wool, worsted weight

Color A: Green, 45 yd. (41m)

Color B: White, 10 yd. (9.1m)

Color C: Gray, 20 yd. (18.2m)

Other supplies

Size 10 US (6mm) knitting needles

Felt (black)

Embroidery floss (black, white, gray, green)

Yarn needle

Embroidery needle

Polyester fiberfill

Flexible craft foam

Polyester pellets, approximately 1 oz. (28g)

Cotton yarn

✪ stitches & techniques

Cast on	Ladder stitch
Bind off	Appliqué stitch
Knit	French knot
Purl	Straight stitch
Make one (M1)	Whipstitch
K2TOG	Backstitch
K3TOG	
Knit Front and Back	
Knit with Multiple Colors	
Felting	

✪ pattern

(EYE)

cut 2

stand mixer

instructions

Mixer Top

Beginning at the top of the mixer, cast on 41 stitches in Color A.

Row 1: K1, KFB, K18, K1, KFB, K18, KFB (44 sts).

Row 2 and all even rows: Purl.

Row 3: K1, (M1, K1) 2 times, K18, (M1, K1) 3 times, K18, M1, K2 (50 sts).

Row 5: K1, (M1, K1) 4 times, K18, (M1, K1) 6 times, K18, (M1, K1) 2 times, K1 (62 sts).

Row 7: K1, (M1, K2) 4 times, K18, (M1, K2) 6 times, K18, (M1, K2) 2 times, K1 (74 sts).

Rows 9–13 (odd only): Knit.

Row 14: Purl.

Continuing in Color B:

Row 15: Knit.

Row 16: Purl.

Row 17: Knit.

Continuing in Color A:

Rows 18 and all even rows: Purl.

Row 19: K1, (K2TOG, K1) 4 times, K18, (K2TOG, K1) 6 times, K18, (K2TOG, K1) 2 times, K1 (62 sts).

Row 21: K1, (K2TOG) 4 times, K18, (K2TOG) 6 times, K18, (K2TOG) 2 times, K1 (50 sts).

Row 23: K1, (K2TOG) 2 times, K18, (K2TOG) 3 times, K18, K2TOG, K1 (44 sts).

Bind off while working K3TOG, K18, K3TOG, K18, K2TOG. Cut the yarn, leaving an 8" (20.3cm) tail. Fold in half with right sides facing and whipstitch the seams together with matching yarn, leaving a 1 1/2" (3.8cm) opening in the bottom of the mixer top. Whipstitch to close the cast-on and bind-off edges, leaving a 1"–1½" (2.5cm–3.8cm) opening in the bottom. The mixer top will be felted separately and attached later.

Mixer Neck

Beginning from the top, cast on 26 stitches in Color A.

Row 1: Knit.

Row 2 and all even rows: Purl.

Row 3: Knit.

Row 5: Knit.

Row 7: K1, (K2TOG, K2) 6 times, K1 (20 sts).

Row 9: Knit.

Row 11: Knit.

Row 13: K1, (M1, K3) 6 times, K1 (26 sts).

Row 15: Knit.

Row 17: Knit.

Row 19: K1, (M1, K4) 6 times, K1 (32 sts).

Row 21: Knit.

Row 23: Knit.

Row 25: K1, (M1, K5) 6 times, K1 (38 sts).

Row 27: Knit.

Row 28: Purl.

Bind off. Whipstitch the seams with matching yarn. The mixer base will be felted separately and attached later.

Mixer Base

Cast on 19 stitches in Color A.

Row 1: Knit.

Row 2 and all even rows: Purl.

Row 3: K1, (M1, K1) 2 times, K4, (M1, K1) 2 times, K1, (M1, K1) 2 times, K4, (M1, K1) 2 times, K1 (27 sts).

Row 5: K1, M1, K12, M1, K1, M1, K12, M1, K1 (31 sts).

Row 7: K1, M1, K14, M1, K1, M1, K14, M1, K1 (35 sts).

Rows 9-43: Knit.

Row 45: K1, K2TOG, K12, K2TOG, K1, K2TOG, K12, K2TOG, K1 (31 sts).

Row 47: K1, K2TOG, K10, K2TOG, K1, K2TOG, K10, K2TOG, K1 (27 sts).

Row 49: K1, K2TOG, K2TOG, K4, K2TOG, K2TOG, K1, K2TOG, K2TOG, K4, K2TOG, K2TOG, K1 (19 sts).

Bind off. Fold the mixer base in half with right sides facing and sew along the selvedge, leaving a 1"–1½" (2.5cm–3.8cm) opening in the side. The mixer base will be felted before assembly.

Bowl

Starting from the top, cast on 38 stitches in Color C.

Rows 1-21: Knit.

Row 2 and All Even Rows: Purl.

Row 23: K1, (K2TOG, K1) 12 times, K1 (26 sts).

Row 25: K1, (K2TOG) 12 times, K1 (14 sts).

Row 27: K1, (K2TOG) 6 times, K1 (8 sts).

Cut the yarn, leaving an 8" (20.3cm) tail. Using a yarn needle, insert the needle through the remaining stitches and pull tight. With right sides facing, whipstitch the seam with matching yarn. The bowl will be assembled *after* felting.

Beater Top

Starting from the outside, cast on 26 stitches in Color C.

Row 1: Knit.

Row 2: Purl.

Row 3: K1, (K2TOG) 12 times, K1 (14 sts).

Row 4: Purl.

Row 5: K1, (K2TOG) 6 times, K1 (8 sts).

Cut the yarn, leaving a 4" (10.2cm) tail. Insert a yarn needle through the remaining stitches and pull tight. With right sides facing, whipstitch the seam with matching yarn. The beater top will be attached *after* felting.

Finishing your stand mixer

Felting

Before you felt your pieces, work in all yarn ends on the wrong side. Check your knitting for any holes and stitch them together loosely with matching yarn. Follow the instructions under Felting Techniques to felt your project.

Shaping

Stuff the mixer top, neck and bowl firmly with fiberfill while damp. Mold the pieces into shape as shown in Diagram 1. Shape the batter and the beater top into flat circles, the beater into a tube and the mixer base into a flat oval. When you are happy with the shapes, let them dry overnight.

detail of eyes

Stuffing and Assembly

When dry, remove temporary stuffing. Fill the bottom of the bowl loosely with polyester pellets as shown in Diagram 1. Stuff the bowl firmly with fresh fiberfill. Use one strand of embroidery thread and a ladder stitch to attach the batter to the bowl. Stuff the mixer top firmly with fiberfill and use two strands of matching embroidery floss with a ladder stitch to close the opening in the bottom of the mixer top. With one strand of matching embroidery floss and the ladder stitch, attach the mixer stand to the mixer base. Fill the bottom of the mixer stand loosely with polyester pellets as shown in Diagram 1. Stuff the mixer stand firmly with fiberfill. Use one strand of matching embroidery floss and a ladder stitch to attach the mixer top. Cut a piece of craft foam as tall as the beater and three times as wide, curve it into a tube and insert it into the beater. Use one strand of embroidery floss and a ladder stitch to attach the beater off center to the batter.

Embroidery

Cut two eyes from black felt. Separate one strand of black embroidery floss and attach the eyes with an appliqué stitch. Using three strands of white embroidery floss, make a French knot and a straight stitch for each eye's highlights. Using three strands of black embroidery floss, backstitch the mouth.

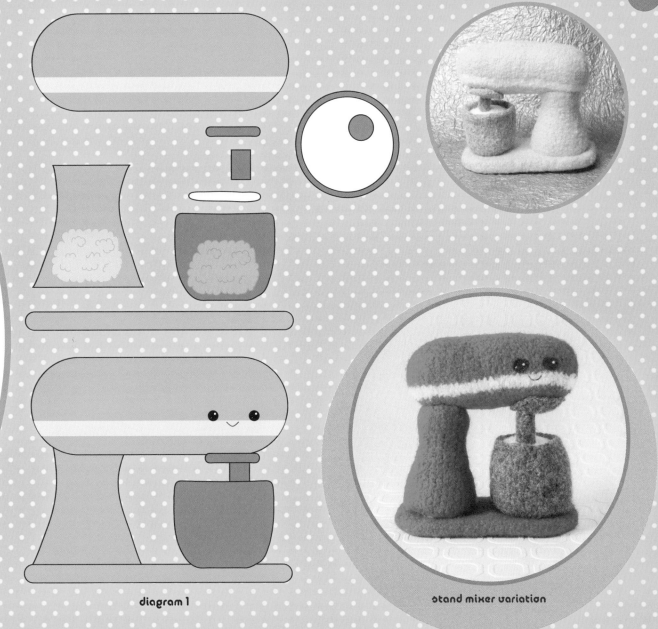

diagram 1

stand mixer variation

CHAPTER THREE

food Fun

⭐ finished size

Approximately 4" (10.2cm) tall, depending on the yarn used and the amount of felting

⭐ materials list

Yarn

100% wool, worsted weight

Color A: Red, 25 yd. (22.8m)

Color B: Brown, 10 yd. (9.1m)

Color C: Leaf Green, 10 yd. (9.1m)

Other supplies

Size 10 US (6mm) knitting needles

Felt (black)

Embroidery floss (black, white, red)

Yarn needle

Embroidery needle

Polyester fiberfill

Polyester pellets, approximately 1 oz. (28g)

Cotton yarn

⭐ stitches & techniques

Cast on	Ladder stitch
Bind off	Appliqué stitch
Knit	French knot
Purl	Straight stitch
Make one (M1)	Whipstitch
K2TOG	Backstitch
K3TOG	
Felting	

⭐ pattern

EYE

cut 2

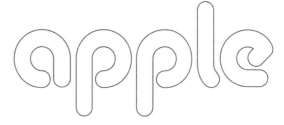

instructions

Apple

Starting from the top of the apple, cast on 8 stitches in Color A.

Row 1: K1, (M1, K1) 6 times, K1 (14 sts).

Row 2 and all even rows: Purl.

Row 3: K1, (M1, K1) 12 times, K1 (26 sts).

Row 5: K1, (M1, K2) 12 times, K1 (38 sts).

Rows 7–15 (odd only): Knit.

Rows 17 & 19: K1, (K2TOG, K2, M1, K1, M1, K2, K2TOG) 4 times, K1 (38 sts).

Row 21: K1, (K3, K3TOG, K3) 4 times, K1 (30 sts).

Row 23: K1, (K2, K3TOG, K2) 4 times, K1 (22 sts).

Row 25: K1, (K1, K3TOG, K1) 4 times, K1 (14 sts).

Row 27: K1, (K2TOG) 6 times, K1 (8 sts).

Cut the yarn, leaving an 8" (20.3cm) tail. Insert a yarn needle through the remaining stitches and pull tight. With right sides facing, whipstitch the seam with matching yarn.

Stem

Cast on 8 stitches in Color B. Bind off. Weave in the ends. The stem will be felted separately and attached later.

Leaf

Starting at the bottom of the leaf, cast on 3 stitches in Color C.

Row 1: Knit.

Row 2 and all even rows: Purl.

Row 3: K1, M1, K1, M1, K1 (5 sts).

Rows 5, 7 and 9: Knit.

Row 11: K2TOG, K1, K2TOG (3 sts).

Row 13: K1, K2TOG (2 sts).

Row 15: K2TOG (1 sts).

Cut the yarn, leaving a 4" (10.2cm) tail. Using a yarn needle, insert the needle through the remaining stitches and pull tight. The leaf will be felted separately and attached later.

Finishing your apple

Felting

Before you felt your apple, stem and leaf, work in all yarn ends on the wrong side. Check your knitting for any holes and stitch them together loosely with matching yarn. Follow the instructions under Felting Techniques to felt your apple.

Shaping

Stuff the apple firmly with fiberfill while damp. Mold it into shape as shown in Diagram 1. The apple should be shaped so that it is wider than it is tall. Shape the leaf into a teardrop and the stem into a rope. When you are happy with the shapes, let them dry overnight.

diagram 1

detail of eyes

Stuffing & Assembly

When completely dry, remove the temporary stuffing. Fill the bottom of the apple loosely with polyester pellets as shown in Diagram 1. Use a ladder stitch to close the opening. Thread the yarn through the bottom center of the apple to the top of the apple and back. Pull to create a small indentation at the base. Repeat two to three times. Sew the stem and the leaf to the center top of the apple as shown in Diagram 1.

Embroidery

Cut two eyes from black felt. Separate one strand of black embroidery floss and attach the eyes with an appliqué stitch. Using three strands of white embroidery floss, make a French knot and a straight stitch for each eye's highlight. Using three strands of black embroidery floss, backstitch the mouth.

apple variation

finished size

Approximately 3"–4" (8.9–10.2cm) wide, depending on the yarn used and the amount of felting

materials list

Yarn

100% wool, worsted weight

Color A: Tan, 15 yd. (13.7m) for small cookie, 20 yd. (18.2m) for large cookie

Color B: Brown, 10 yd. (9.1m)

Other supplies

Size 10 US (6mm) knitting needles

Felt (black)

Embroidery floss (black, white)

Yarn needle

Embroidery needle

stitches & techniques

Cast on

Bind off

Knit

Purl

Make one (M1)

K2TOG

Felting

Appliqué stitch

Chain stitch

French knot

Straight stitch

Whipstitch

Backstitch

pattern

EYE
cut 2

chocolate chip cookies

instructions

Small Cookie

Starting at the bottom of the cookie on the wrong side, cast on 8 stitches in Color A.

Row 1 and all odd rows: Purl.

Row 2: K1, (M1, K1) 6 times, K1 (14 sts).

Row 4: K1, (M1, K1) 12 times, K1 (26 sts).

Row 6: K1, (M1, K2) 12 times, K1 (38 sts).

Row 8: K1, (K2TOG, K1) 12 times, K1 (26 sts).

Row 10: K1, (K2TOG) 12 times, K1 (14 sts).

Row 12: K1, (K2TOG) 6 times, K1 (8 sts).

Cut the yarn, leaving a 4" (10.2cm) tail. Insert a yarn needle through the remaining stitches and pull tight. With the cookies inside out, whipstitch the seams with matching yarn, leaving the bottom cast-on edge open. Turn right side out. Weave the yarn through the stitches on the cast-on edge to gather. Pull tightly, secure and weave in the ends. Chain stitch the chocolate chips in Color B on the top surface of your cookie.

Large Cookie

Starting at the bottom of the cookie on the wrong side, cast on 8 stitches in Color A.

Row 1 and all odd rows: Purl.

Row 2: K1, (M1, K1) 6 times, K1 (14 sts).

Row 4: K1, (M1, K1) 12 times, K1 (26 sts).

Row 6: K1, (M1, K2) 12 times, K1 (38 sts).

Row 8: K1, (M1, K3) 12 times, K1 (50 sts).

Row 10: K1, (K2TOG, K2) 12 times, K1 (38 sts).

Row 12: K1, (K2TOG, K1) 12 times, K1 (26 sts).

Row 14: K1, (K2TOG) 12 times, K1 (14 sts).

Row 16: K1, (K2TOG) 6 times, K1 (8 sts).

Cut the yarn, leaving an 8" (20.3cm) tail. Insert a yarn needle through the remaining stitches and pull tight. With the cookies inside out, whipstitch the seams with matching yarn, leaving the bottom cast-on edge open. Turn right side out. Weave the yarn through the stitches on the cast-on edge to gather. Pull tightly, secure and weave in ends. Chain stitch the chocolate chips in Color B on the top surface of your cookie.

finishing your cookies

Felting

Before you felt your cookies, work in all yarn ends on the wrong side. Check your knitting for any holes and stitch them together loosely with matching yarn. Follow the instructions under Felting Techniques to felt your cookies.

Shaping

Shape the cookie into a circle as shown in Diagram 1. When you are happy with the shape, let it dry overnight.

Embroidery

Cut two eyes from black felt. Separate one strand of black embroidery floss and attach the eyes with an appliqué stitch. Using three strands of white embroidery floss, make a French knot and a straight stitch for each eye's highlights. With three strands of black embroidery floss, backstitch the mouth.

detail of eyes

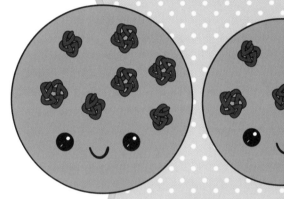

diagram 1

chocolate chip cookie variation

⭐ finished size

Approximately 4½" (11.3cm) tall, depending on the yarn used and the amount of felting

⭐ materials list

yarn

100% wool, worsted weight

Color A: White, 15 yd. (13.7m)

Color B: Orange, 25 yd. (22.8m)

Color C: Green, 10 yd. (9.1m)

Color D: Gold, 10 yd. (9.1m)

Other supplies

Size 10 US (6mm) knitting needles

Felt (black)

Embroidery floss (black, white, orange, green gold)

Yarn needle

Embroidery needle

Polyester fiberfill

Polyester pellets, approximately 1 oz. (28g)

Cotton yarn to temporarily secure seams

⭐ stitches & techniques

Cast on	Ladder stitch
Bind off	Appliqué stitch
Knit	French knot
Purl	Straight stitch
Make one (M1)	Whipstitch
K2TOG	Backstitch
K3TOG	
Knit with multiple colors	
Felting	

⭐ pattern

EYE
cut 2

instructions

Cut the yarn, leaving an 8" (20.3cm) tail. Insert a yarn needle through the remaining stitches and pull tight. With right sides facing, whipstitch the seam with matching yarn.

Bottle

Beginning at the top, cast on 9 stitches in Color A.

Row 1: Knit.

Row 2 and all even rows: Purl.

Row 3: Knit.

Row 5: Knit.

Row 6: Purl.

Continuing in Color B:

Row 7: K1, (M1, K1) 7 times, K1 (16 sts).

Row 9: K1, (M1, K2) 7 times, K1 (23 sts).

Row 11: K1, (M1, K3) 7 times, K1 (30 sts).

Row 13: Knit.

Row 15: Knit.

Row 17: K1, (K2TOG, K2) 7 times, K1 (23 sts).

Continuing in Color A:

Row 18: Purl.

Row 19–29 (odd only): Knit.

Row 30: Purl.

Continuing in Color B:

Row 31: K1, (M1, K3) 7 times, K1 (30 sts).

Row 33: Knit.

Row 35: Knit.

Row 37: (K2TOG, K1) 10 times (20 sts).

Row 39: (K2TOG) 10 times (10 sts).

Bottle Cap

Beginning at the bottom, cast on 12 stitches in Color C.

Row 1: Knit.

Row 2: Purl.

Row 3: Knit.

Row 4: Purl.

Row 5: K1, (K2TOG) 5 times, K1 (7 sts).

Cut the yarn, leaving a 4" (10.2cm) tail. Insert a yarn needle through the remaining stitches and pull tight. With right sides facing, whipstitch the seam with matching yarn. The cap will be felted separately and attached later.

Orange Slice

Beginning on the wrong side, cast on 20 stitches in Color D.

Row 1: Purl.

Continuing in Color B:

Row 2: K1, (K2TOG, K1) 6 times, K1 (14 sts).

Row 3: Purl.

Row 4: K1, (K2TOG) 6 times, K1 (8 sts).

Row 5: Purl.

Row 6: (K2TOG) 3 times, K1 (5 sts).

Cut the yarn, leaving an 8" (20.3cm) tail. Insert a yarn needle through the remaining stitches and pull tight. Weave in the ends. Attach the orange slice to the bottle as shown in Diagram 1 before felting. Straight stitch the orange segments onto the orange slice using Color D.

detail of eyes

diagram 1

Finishing your orange soda

Felting

Before you felt your bottle and cap, work in all the yarn ends on the wrong side. Check your knitting for any holes and stitch them together loosely with matching yarn. Follow the instructions under Felting Techniques to felt your project.

Shaping

Stuff the bottle firmly with fiberfill while damp. Mold the pieces into shape as shown in Diagram 1. The bottle should be shaped so that it is wider than it is tall. Shape the cap into a cylinder. When you are happy with the shapes, let them dry overnight.

Stuffing

When completely dry, remove the temporary stuffing. Fill the bottom of the bottle loosely with polyester pellets as shown in Diagram 1, then stuff firmly. Use a ladder stitch to close the opening. Thread the yarn through the bottom center of the bottle to the top of the bottle and back, then pull to create a small indentation at the base. Repeat two or three times. Place the cap on the bottle or attach with a ladder stitch.

Embroidery

Cut two eyes from black felt. Separate one strand from black embroidery floss and attach the eyes with an appliqué stitch. Using three strands of white embroidery floss, make a french knot and a straight stitch for each eye's highlights. Using three strands of black embroidery floss, backstitch the mouth.

orange soda variation

finished size

Approximately 4" (10.2cm) tall, depending on the yarn used and the amount of felting

materials list

Yarn

100% wool, worsted weight

Color A: White, 40 yd. (36.4m)

Color B: Pink, 45 yd. (41m)

Other supplies

Size 10 US (6mm) knitting needles

Felt (black)

Embroidery floss (black, white, pink)

Yarn needle

Embroidery needle

Polyester fiberfill

Polyester pellets, approximately 1 oz. (28g)

Cotton yarn

stitches & techniques

Cast on

Bind off

Knit

Purl

Make one (M1)

K2TOG

Knit front and back

Pick up stitches

Knit with multiple colors

Felting

Ladder stitch

Appliqué stitch

French knot

Straight stitch

Whipstitch

Backstitch

pattern

EYE

cut 2

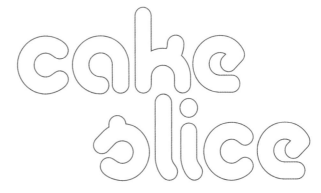

cake slice

instructions

Cake Sides (Make 2)

Beginning at the bottom, cast on 22 stitches in Color A.

Row 1–9 (odd only): Knit.
Row 2–8 (even only): Purl.
Continuing in Color B:
Row 10: Purl.
Row 11: Knit.
Continuing in Color A:
Rows 12–22 (even only): Purl.
Rows 13–21 (odd only): Knit.

Bind off, weave in the ends. Cut the yarn, leaving an 8" (20.3cm) tail. Whipstitch the bottom to the icing (Color A). Whipstitch cake side 1 to cake side 2 and back icing. Weave in the ends on the wrong side.

Back Icing

Beginning at the bottom, cast on 14 stitches in Color B.

Rows 1–21 (odd only): Knit.
Rows 2–22 (even only): Purl.

Bind off. Cut the yarn, leaving an 8" (20.3cm) tail. Whipstitch the bottom to the icing (Color A). Weave in ends on the wrong side.

Icing (Make 1 Color A and 1 Color B)

Beginning at the back, cast on 14 stitches.

Row 1: Knit.
Row 2 and all even rows: Purl.
Row 3: Knit.
Row 5: K1, K2TOG, K8, K2TOG, K1 (12 sts).
Row 7: Knit.
Row 9: K1, K2TOG, K6, K2TOG, K1 (10 sts).
Row 11: Knit.
Row 13: K1, K2TOG, K4, K2TOG, K1 (8 sts).
Row 15: Knit.
Row 17: K1, K2TOG, K2, K2TOG, K1 (6 sts).
Row 19: Knit.
Row 21: K1, K2TOG, K2TOG, K1 (4 sts).
Row 23: Knit.
Row 24: Purl.

Cut the yarn, leaving a 4" (10.2cm) tail. Insert a yarn needle through the remaining stitches and pull tight. Whipstitch the icing (Color B) to the top of the cake sides and back icing, leaving a 1½" (3.8cm) opening in the back.

Shell Border (Make 4)

Beginning from the side, cast on 4 stitches in Color B.

Row 1: Knit.
Row 2: (KFB) 4 times (8 sts).
Row 3: (KFB, K1) 4 times (12 sts).
Row 4: Knit.
Row 5: (K1, K2TOG) 4 times (8 sts).

Row 6: (K2TOG) 4 times (4 sts).

Row 7: (K2TOG) 2 times (2 sts).

Row 8: (KFB) 2 times (4 sts).

Row 9: (KFB) 4 times (8 sts).

Row 10: (KFB, K1) 4 times (12 sts).

Row 11: Knit.

Row 12: (K1, K2TOG) 4 times (8 sts).

Row 13: (K2TOG) 4 times (4 sts).

Row 14: (K2TOG) 2 times (2 sts).

Row 15: (KFB) 2 times (4 sts).

Row 16: (KFB) 4 times (8 sts).

Row 17: (KFB, K1) 4 times (12 sts).

Row 18: Knit.

Row 19: (K1, K2TOG) 4 times (8 sts).

Row 20: (K2TOG) 4 times (4 sts).

Row 21: (K2TOG) 2 times (2 sts).

Row 22: (KFB) 2 times (4 sts).

Cut the yarn, leaving a 4" (10.2cm) tail. Insert a yarn needle through the remaining stitches and pull tight. The shell borders will be felted separately and attached later.

detail of eyes

diagram 1

finishing your cake slice

Felting
Before you felt your cake slice, work in all the yarn ends on the wrong side. With colorfast cotton yarn, baste to close the opening on the back of the cake. Check your knitting for any holes and stitch them together loosely with matching yarn. Follow the instructions under Felting Techniques to felt your cake slice and shell border pieces.

Shaping
Stuff the cake slice firmly with fiberfill while damp. Mold into a wedge shape as shown in Diagram 1. Using pins, pinch then pin all edges and corners to sharpen them. The shell border pieces should be dried flat. When you are happy with the shapes, let them dry overnight.

Stuffing and Assembly
When completely dry, remove the temporary stuffing. Fill the bottom of the cake slice loosely with polyester pellets. Use matching embroidery floss and a ladder stitch to close the opening. Using two shell border pieces, fold each piece in half lengthwise and stack, then sew to the bottom and top edges as shown in Diagram 1.

Embroidery
Cut two eyes from black felt. Separate one strand of black embroidery floss and attach the eyes with an appliqué stitch. Using three strands of white embroidery floss, make a French knot and a straight stitch for each eye's highlights. Using three strands of black embroidery floss, backstitch the mouth.

cake slice variation

Finished size

Approximately 7" (17.8cm) tall, depending on the yarn used and the amount of felting

Materials List

Yarn

100% wool, worsted weight

Color A: Pink, 20 yd. (18.2m)

Color B: Gray, 40 yd. (36.4m)

Color C: White, 25 yd. (22.8m)

Color D: Brown, 15 yd. (13.7m)

Color E: Red, 10 yd. (9.1m)

Other supplies

Size 10 US (6mm) knitting needles

Felt (black)

Embroidery floss (black, white, pink, brown, red)

Yarn needle

Embroidery needle

Polyester fiberfill

Polyester pellets, approximately 1 oz. (28g)

Cotton yarn

Stitches & techniques

Cast on	Ladder stitch
Bind off	Appliqué stitch
Knit	French knot
Purl	Straight stitch
Make one (M1)	Whipstitch
K2TOG	Backstitch
Wrap and turn	
Felting	

Pattern

EYE

cut 2

instructions

Ice Cream Scoop

Beginning at the top, cast on 8 stitches in Color A.

Row 1: Knit.

Row 2 and all even rows: Purl.

Row 3: K1, (M1, K1) 6 times, K1 (14 sts).

Row 5: K1, (M1, K1) 12 times, K1 (26 sts).

Row 7: K1, (M1, K2) 12 times, K1 (38 sts).

Row 9: Knit.

Row 11: Knit.

Row 13: Knit.

Row 15: K1, (K2TOG, K1) 12 times, K1 (26 sts).

Row 17: K1, (K2TOG) 12 times, K1 (14 sts).

Row 19: K1, (K2TOG) 6 times, K1 (8 sts).

Cut the yarn, leaving an 8" (20.3cm) tail. Insert a yarn needle through the remaining stitches and pull tight. With right sides facing, whipstitch the seam with matching yarn, leaving the bottom cast-on edge open. Weave in the ends on the wrong side. The ice cream scoop will be felted separately and attached later.

Ice Cream Filler

Beginning on the wrong side, cast on 38 stitches in Color C.

Row 1: Purl.

Row 2: K1, (K2TOG, K1) 12 times, K1 (26 sts).

Row 3: Purl.

Row 4: K1, (K2TOG) 12 times, K1 (14 sts).

Row 5: Purl.

Row 6: K1, (K2TOG) 6 times, K1 (8 sts).

Cut the yarn, leaving a 4" (10.2cm) tail. Insert a yarn needle through the remaining stitches and pull tight. With right sides facing, whipstitch the seam with matching yarn. The ice cream filler will be felted separately and attached later.

Dish

Beginning at the top, cast on 38 stitches in Color B.

Row 1: Knit.

Row 2 and all even rows: Purl.

Row 3: K1, (K2TOG, K4) 6 times, K1 (32 sts).

Row 5: K1, (K2TOG, K3) 6 times, K1 (26 sts).

Row 7: Knit.

Row 9: K1, (M1, K4) 6 times, K1 (32 sts).

Row 11: Knit.

Row 13: K1, (M1, K5) 6 times, K1 (38 sts).

detail of eyes

Row 15: Knit.
Row 17: Knit.
Row 19: Knit.
Row 21: Knit.
Row 23: K1, (K2TOG, K1) 12 times, K1 (26 sts).
Row 25: K1, (K2TOG) 12 times, K1 (14 sts).
Row 27: K1, (M1, K2) 6 times, K1(20 sts).
Row 29: K1, (M1, K3) 6 times, K1 (26 sts).
Row 31: K1, (M1, K2) 12 times, K1 (38 sts).
Row 33: K1, (K2TOG, K1) 12 times, K1 (26 sts).
Row 35: K1, (K2TOG) 12 times, K1 (14 sts).
Row 37: K1, (K2TOG) 6 times, K1 (8 sts).
Cut the yarn, leaving an 8" (20.3cm) tail. Insert a yarn needle through the remaining stitches and pull tight. With right sides facing, whipstitch the seam with matching yarn. Weave in the ends on the wrong side. The dish will be felted separately and attached later.

Whipped Cream

Beginning at the bottom, cast on 12 stitches in Color C.
Row 1: Knit.
Row 2 and all even rows: Purl.
Row 3: K1, (M1, K1) 12 times, K1 (26 sts).
Row 5: K1, (M1, K4) 6 times, K1 (32 sts).
Row 7: K1, (K2TOG, K3) 6 times, K1 (26 sts).
Row 9: K1, (K2TOG) 12 times, K1 (14 sts).
Row 11: K1, (M1, K2) 6 times, K1 (20 sts).
Row 13: K1, (M1, K3) 8 times, K1 (26 sts).

Row 15: K1, (K2TOG, K1) 8 times, K1 (18 sts).
Row 17: K1, (K2TOG) 8 times, K1 (10 sts).
Cut the yarn, leaving an 8" (20.3cm) tail. Insert a yarn needle through the remaining stitches and pull tight. With right sides facing, whipstitch the seam with matching yarn, leaving the bottom cast-on edge open. Weave in the ends on the wrong side. The whipped cream will be felted separately and attached later.

Fudge

Cast on 8 stitches in Color D.
Row 1: K6, wrap and turn (8 sts).
Row 2: Knit (8 sts).
Row 3: Bind off 3, K2, wrap and turn (5 sts).
Row 4: Knit. Cast on 5 (10 sts).
Row 5: K6, wrap and turn (10 sts).
Row 6: Knit (10 sts).
Row 7: Bind off 5, knit (5 sts).
Row 8: Knit. Cast on 3 (8 sts).
Repeat Rows 1–8 four more times, then repeat rows 1–6.
Bind off. Insert a yarn needle through the remaining stitches and pull tight. Whipstitch the seams with matching yarn and weave in the ends on the wrong side. The fudge will be attached *after* felting.

Cherry

Beginning at the bottom, cast on 8 stitches in Color E.

Row 1: Knit.

Row 2: K1, (M1, K1) 6 times, K1 (14 sts).

Row 3: Knit.

Row 4: Knit.

Row 5: K1, (K2TOG) 6 times (8 sts).

Cut the yarn, leaving a 4" (10.2cm) tail. Insert a yarn needle through the remaining stitches and pull tight. With right sides facing, whipstitch the seam with matching yarn. The cherry will be felted separately and attached later.

Finishing your ice cream sundae

Felting

Before you felt your ice cream sundae pieces, work in all the yarn ends on the wrong side. Check your knitting for any holes and stitch them together loosely with matching yarn. Using a colorsafe cotton yarn, baste to close the opening on the back. Follow the instructions under Felting Techniques to felt your sundae.

Shaping

Remove the cotton yarn from the opening at the back and stuff the ice cream scoop, dish, whipped cream and cherry firmly with fiberfill while damp. Mold them into shape as shown in Diagram 1. The ice cream scoop should be shaped so that it is wider than it is tall. Shape the ice cream filler into a flat circle. When you are happy with the shapes, let them dry overnight.

Stuffing and Assembly

When completely dry, remove the temporary stuffing. Fill the bottom of the dish loosely with polyester pellets as shown in Diagram 1. Use one strand of matching thread and a ladder stitch to attach the ice cream filler to the dish, stuffing firmly with fiberfill. Use one strand of matching embroidery thread and a ladder stitch to attach the ice cream filler to the dish. Thread the yarn through the bottom center of the dish to the center of the ice cream filler and back (if you cannot reach, then do so at the indention of the glass to make a more pronounced base). Pull to create a small indentation at the base and repeat two or three times. Stuff the ice cream scoop, whipped cream and cherry firmly with fiberfill. Close the seams with a ladder stitch and matching thread. Attach all pieces as shown in Diagram 1, using a ladder stitch and matching embroidery thread.

Embroidery

Cut two eyes from black felt. Separate one strand from black embroidery floss and attach eyes with appliqué stitch as shown in Diagram 2. Using three strands of white embroidery floss, make a French knot and straight stitch for each eye's highlights. Using three strands of black embroidery floss, backstitch the mouth.

diagram 1

ice cream sundae variation

materials

All of the materials used to make these adorable projects can be purchased at any craft store.

When choosing which wool yarn to use when knitting your amigurumi, be certain to purchase 100% wool, otherwise you will not be able to felt your pieces at the end.

Fill a small container or dishpan with about 1" (2.5cm) of hot water. Add a small amount of dish soap. Place the project body and parts into the water and let them soak for about five minutes. This will open up the wool fibers for felting. Vigorously squish each piece. Repeat until the individual knitted stitches are not visible. If the pieces get too sudsy, rinse to check your progress.

Some colors may felt faster than others. If you are having trouble felting your pieces, try using gloves with rubber beads on the palms to help agitate the wool. If you are concerned that some colors may bleed in the hot water, either do a text swatch before placing you project in the tub, or felt each color separately.

make samples!

White wool is often more difficult to felt than colored wool due to the process used to whiten it. Test a sample of the wool you plan to use before making your project to ensure you will get the results you desire.

Fabric before it is felted.

Fabric after it is felted.

knitting techniques

cast on

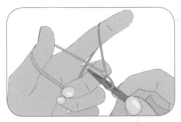

1 Make a slip knot, leaving a long tail (about 4" [10.2cm] for every 1" [2.5cm] you'll be casting on). Slide the slip knot onto the needle with the long tail toward the front of the needle. Slide your thumb and index finger between the two strands of yarn. Wrap the long tail around your thumb and the strand still attached to the skein around your index finger. Grasp both strands with your remaining fingers.

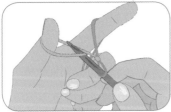

2 Slide the tip of the needle up through the yarn wrapped around your thumb.

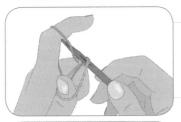

3 Keeping the needle in the loop of yarn around the thumb, hook the needle behind the strand of yarn on the front of your index finger.

4 Bring the yarn through the loop of yarn on your thumb, creating a second loop on your needle (the first cast-on stitch). Gently tug on the strands with your thumb and index finger to tighten the cast-on stitch. Repeat to cast on the remaining stitches. Include the slip knot in your stitch count.

three-color cast on

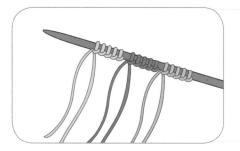

1 To cast on multiple colors, cast on the desired number of stitches for Color A, then release that color. Cast on the desired number of stitches for Color B, then release that color. Do the same for color C unless you are returning to Color A. If reusing Color A as the third color, cast on the desired number of stitches from a separate length or ball of yarn. Tails should hang to the left when casting on, but will be on the right when you turn the needle to begin working.

change colors (at end of row)

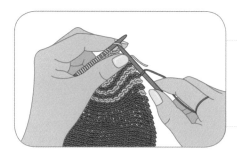

1 To change colors at the end of a row, drop Color A before beginning the next row. Begin the next row as usual, but pick up Color B and begin knitting with it while leaving Color A unused. The previous color can be trimmed, leaving a 6" (15.2cm) tail.

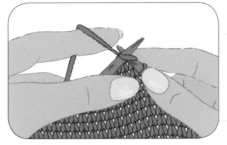

knit (continental style)

1 With the working yarn wrapped over your left index finger, insert the right-hand needle into the first stitch on the left-hand needle from front to back. The right-hand needle should cross behind the left-hand needle.

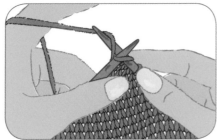

2 Bring the right-hand needle tip behind the yarn in front of your left index finger. The working yarn should be wrapped around the right needle tip counterclockwise.

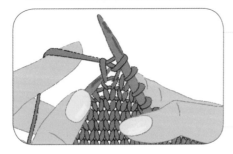

3 Dip the needle tip down and pull the wrapped yarn through the stitch on the left-hand needle. Bring the yarn up on the right-hand needle to create a new stitch, allowing the old stitch to slide easily off the left-hand needle. The new stitch remains on the right-hand needle.

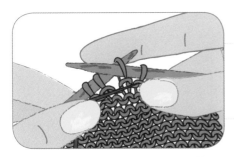

purl

1 With the working yarn in your left hand, slide the tip of the right-hand needle into the first stitch on the left-hand needle from back to front. The right-hand needle should cross in front of the left-hand needle.

2 Use your left hand to wrap the working yarn around the tip of the right-hand needle counterclockwise. Draw the right-hand needle back through the stitch on the left-hand needle, catching the wrapped working yarn with the tip of the needle. Bring the working yarn through the stitch on the left-hand needle.

3 Bring the yarn up on the right-hand needle to create a new stitch, allowing the old stitch to slide off the left-hand needle. The new stitch remains on the right-hand needle.

For illustration purposes, the working yarn is shown held between the index finger and thumb. However, when working a row of purl stitches, the yarn should remain in the position shown in step 2 to create proper tension.

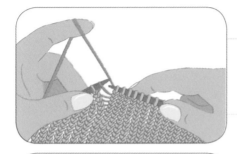

make one (m1)

1 Bring the tip of the left-hand needle under the strand between stitches from front to back.

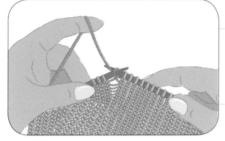

2 Insert the tip of the right-hand needle through the back of the yarn sitting on the left-hand needle.

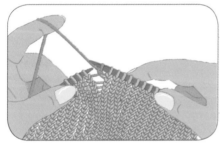

3 Knit this strand through the back loop to twist it. The right-hand needle should now have a new stitch. This will increase your stitch count by one stitch.

knit 2 together (k2tog)

Place your needle tip through two stitches instead of one. Knit the stitches together into a single stitch.

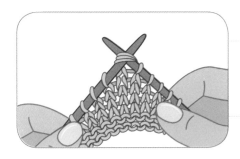

knit 3 together (k3tog)

Place your needle tip through three stitches instead of one. Knit the stitches together into a single stitch.

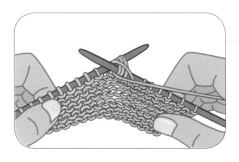

purl 2 together (p2tog)

Place your needle tip through two stitches instead of one, purlwise. Purl the stitches together into a single stitch.

knit front and back (kfb)

1 Slip the right-hand needle into the first stitch on the left-hand needle from front to back and knit the stitch as usual, but do not slip the stitch off of the left-hand needle.

2 Insert the right-hand needle through the back of the same stitch and knit another stitch.

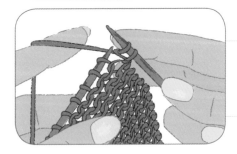

3 Slide the old stitch off of the left-hand needle. The right-hand needle should now have two new stitches. This will increase your stitch count by one stitch.

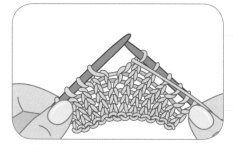

wrap and turn

1 Knit to where you want to begin shaping. With the yarn in the back, slip the next stitch purlwise from the left needle to the right needle and bring the yarn to the front between the needles.

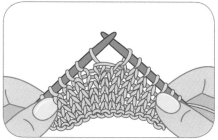

2 Slip the last stitch on the right needle back to the left needle and bring the yarn to the back. The wrap will show on the stitch. Turn the work and purl to the other end of the shaping section or to the end of the row.

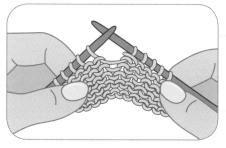

3 Purl to the place you want to begin shaping. With the yarn in the front, slip the next stitch purlwise from the left needle to the right needle and then bring the yarn to the back between the needles.

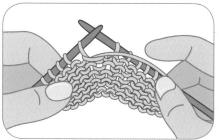

4 Slip the last stitch on the right needle back to the left needle. Turn the work and, with the yarn in the position to knit the next stitch, work to the other end of the shaping section or to the end of the row.

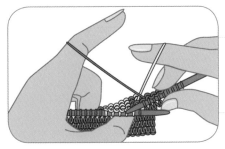

intarsia (color change)

1 If you're knitting a block of Color A and you want to continue in Color B, twist the yarns by bringing Color B under Color A, then knit the stitch with Color B.

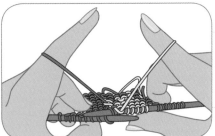

2 If you're knitting a block of Color B and want to knit the next stitch on top of Color A as Color B, just continue to knit with Color B. To work with Color A on the next stitch, bring the Color A yarn over the Color B yarn and continue.

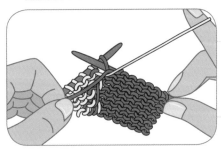

3 If you're purling with Color A and want to continue in Color B, bring the Color B yarn under the Color A yarn, then purl the stitch with Color B.

4 On the other side, if you're purling a block of Color B and want to purl the first stitch of the next color block in Color A, purl the stitch with Color B and then pick up Color A over Color B and continue. This image shows the Color B stitch already purled and the Color A yarn being placed over it to continue.

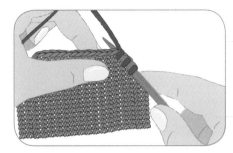

pick up stitches

1 Insert the tip of the knitting needle under a stitch on the finished edge of the knitted fabric. Be careful to pick up both strands of yarn from the stitch.

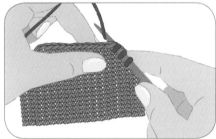

2 Wrap the working yarn around the tip of the needle counterclockwise, just as when knitting.

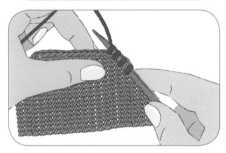

3 Using the tip of the needle, pull the yarn through the knitted fabric, creating a new stitch on the needle. Continue picking up stitches until the appropriate number of stitches is on your needle.

bind off

1 Knit the first two stitches in the row just as you would for a normal knitted row.

2 Insert the left-hand needle into the first knitted stitch on the right-hand needle then pass it over the second knitted stitch on the right-hand needle.

3 One stitch will remain on the right-hand needle.

4 To bind off the next stitch, knit one stitch (two stitches on right-hand needle), then pass the preceding stitch over the newly knitted stitch. Continue to knit one stitch and then pass the preceding stitch over it until you have bound off all of the stitches. Cut the yarn and pull the tail through the final stitch.

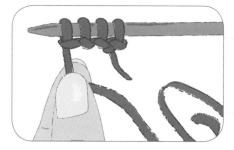

i-cord

1 Cast on the required number of stitches onto one double-pointed needle.

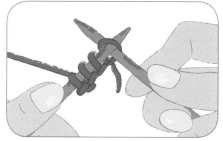

2 Slide the stitches on the double-pointed needle so that the first cast-on stitch is at the right-hand point of the double-pointed needle and the working yarn is to the left of the stitches. Insert another double-pointed needle into the first cast-on stitch.

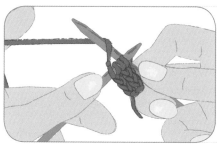

3 Pull the working yarn from the last stitch to the first stitch and knit. Knit all the stitches in the first row. Instead of turning the needle when you finish a row as you would for regular knitting, simply slide all the stitches from the left point to the right point of the needle again. Do not turn your work at all while knitting I-cord. After a few rows, you will see the beginning of a knitted tube.

embroidery techniques

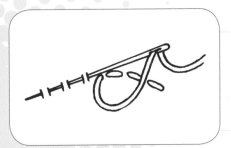

straight stitch

To embroider a line of straight stitches, bring the needle up through the fabric at your desired starting point. Insert the needle into the end position of the first stitch in the series, then up through the fabric at the starting point of the next stitch. Repeat until the line of stitches is the length you desire.

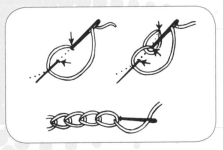

chain stitch

Bring the thread to the right side of the fabric and hold the thread toward you with your left thumb. Take a stitch into the same hole where the thread was brought up, forming a small loop. Do not pull thread tightly. Bring the needle out a short distance forward and over the loop. Make a second loop overlapping the first one. Continue as desired.

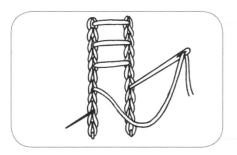

ladder stitch

Make two parallel rows of chain stitch, then join these by making a long, single stitch through the center of each chain stitch.

When using the ladder stitch in knitting, the "chain stitch" is already made for you—it is the V along the edge of the knitted fabric. Insert your thread or yarn through the center of the Vs on each side and pull tight to close.

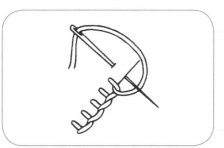

appliqué stitch

Draw thread through at the desired distance from the edge of the piece you are going to appliqué. Hold the thread at left toward you. Thrust the needle through the fabric to the desired depth and draw toward you, passing it over the thread. Draw it up until the purl of thread lies along the edge of the appliqué. Keep the stitches evenly spaced.

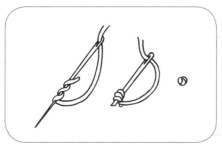

french knot

Bring the needle up through the fabric. Wrap the thread around the tip of the needle the desired number of times and then thrust the needle downward one or two fabric threads away from where it was brought up. Draw the thread through carefully to form a knot on the right side of your fabric.

index

O

Orange Soda, 2, 10, 81, 90-95

P

pick up stitches, 119
plant projects. See Cactus; Topiary
Puppy, 5, 12, 14-19
purl, 113
purl 2 together, 115

R

Rag Doll Kitten, 6, 13, 20-25, 127
Robot, 2, 49, 62-67

S

shaping. See specific projects
Sock Monkey, 3, 48, 68-73
Stand Mixer, 74-79
stitches, embroidery, 15, 21, 27, 31,
    37, 43, 51, 57, 63, 69, 75, 83, 87,
    91, 97, 103, 122-123
straight stitch, 122
    See also specific projects
stuffing. See specific projects

T

Topiary, 5, 10, 48, 56-61

W

wrap and turn, 117

Y

yarn, wool, 8, 108, 109
    See also specific projects;
    knitting techniques

There are many companies
that make 100% wool
yarn. Here are a few:

Cascade Yarns
www.cascadeyarns.com

Patons Yarn
www.patonsyarns.com

Lion Brand Yarn
www.lionbrand.com

Bernat
www.bernat.com

Red Heart
www.redheart.com

Debbie Bliss
www.debbieblissonline.com

acknowledgements

Many thanks to Megumi Kinjo, without whom these projects could not have been completed so quickly.

Thanks, also, to editor Noel Rivera who worked hard to make this book a reality.

about the author

Lisa Eberhart is the creator of www.craftyalien.com, the home of her fantastic knitted and crocheted amigurumi designs.

metric conversion chart

TO CONVERT	TO	MULTIPLY BY
Inches	Centimeters	2.54
Centimeters	Inches	0.4
Feet	Centimeters	30.5
Centimeters	Feet	0.03
Yards	Meters	0.9
Meters	Yards	1.1

THAT'S THE TAIL END, FOLKS!

Felted Knit Amigurumi. Copyright © 2013 by Lisa Eberhart. Manufactured in China. All rights reserved. No part of this book may be reproduced in any form or by any electronic or mechanical means including information storage and retrieval systems without permission in writing from the publisher, except by a reviewer who may quote brief passages in a review. Published by KP Craft, an imprint of F+W Media, Inc., 10151 Carver Road, Ste. 200, Cincinnati, OH 45242. (800) 289-0963. First Edition.

www.fwmedia.com

Other fine KP Craft books are available from your favorite bookstore, art supply store or online supplier. Visit our website at www.fwmedia.com.

17 16 15 14 13   5 4 3 2 1

Distributed in Canada by Fraser Direct
100 Armstrong Avenue
Georgetown, ON, Canada L7G 5S4
Tel: (905) 877-4411

Distributed in the U.K. and Europe
by F&W Media International LTD
Brunel House, Forde Close, Newton Abbot, Devon,
TQ12 4PU, UK
Tel: (+44) 1626 323200
Fax: (+44) 1626 323319
Email: enquiries@fwmedia.com

Distributed in Australia by Capricorn Link
P.O. Box 704, S. Windsor, NSW 2756 Australia
Tel: (02) 4560-1600
Fax: (02) 4577-5288
Email: books@capricornlink.com.au

Edited by *Noel Rivera*

Designed by *Kelly Pace*

Photographed by *Jeff Lyon Photography and Steven Siedentopf of Luna Root Studio*

Project variations knitted by *Megumi Kinjo*

Production coordinated by *Greg Nock*

adorable. colorful. Fun!

happy stitch

30 Felt & Fabric Projects for Everyday
by Jodie Rackley

These thirty charming and achievable projects are not only adorable, they're useful too! Great as gifts or as personal, everyday items, the clear step-by-step illustrations and instructions will make creating these whimsical projects a joy.

ISBN-13: 978-1-4403-1857-3
SRN: W6014

Knitted toy tales

Irresistible Characters for All Ages
by Laura Long

Knitted Toy Tales offers knitters a unique spin on knitted characters, allowing them to build their own individual collection. These twenty adorable, colorful characters are packed with charm and great for gift giving or as quirky home accents.

ISBN-13: 978-0-7153-3172-9
SRN: Z4297

CHECK OUT OUR OTHER KNITTING BOOKS AT KNITTINGDAILY.COM!